Bronc Busters
and Hay Sloops

BRONC BUSTERS and HAY SLOOPS

RANCHING IN THE WEST IN THE EARLY 20TH CENTURY

KEN MATHER

VANCOUVER · VICTORIA · CALGARY

Heritage House Publishing Company Ltd.
www.heritagehouse.ca

Library and Archives Canada Cataloguing in Publication

Mather, Ken, 1947–
   Bronc busters and hay sloops: ranching in the West in the early 20th century / Ken Mather.

Includes bibliographical references and index.

ISBN 978-1-894974-92-9

   1. Ranching—British Columbia—History—20th century. 2. Frontier and pioneer life—British Columbia. 3. Ranchers—British Columbia—Anecdotes. 4. Women ranchers—British Columbia—Anecdotes. 5. Cowboys—British Columbia—Anecdotes. I. Title.

SF196.C2M36 2010   971.1'041   C2009-907543-1

Edited by Lesley Cameron
Proofread by Holland Gidney
Cover design by Jacqui Thomas
Interior design by Darlene Nickull
Front cover: Native Okanagan cowboys Gabriel Paul and Alec Jack, Okanagan Archives
   Trust, Stocks Collection
Back cover: Chilco Ranch haying crew, 1920s, Museum of the Cariboo Chilcotin, Williams
   Lake photo
Maps by Ken Mather

Mixed Sources
Cert no. SW-COC-001271
© 1996 FSC
FSC

The interior of this book was produced on 100% post-consumer recycled paper, processed chlorine free and printed with vegetable-based inks.

Heritage House acknowledges the financial support for its publishing program from the Government of Canada through the Canada Book Fund (CBF), Canada Council for the Arts and the province of British Columbia through the British Columbia Arts Council and the Book Publishing Tax Credit.

Canada Council   Conseil des Arts
for the Arts   du Canada

BRITISH COLUMBIA
ARTS COUNCIL
Supported by the Province of British Columbia

Printed in Canada

CONTENTS

ACKNOWLEDGEMENTS

I would like to dedicate this book to the memory of my late wife, Sandra Anne Mather, whose support and devotion for 30 years allowed me to pursue my interest in history.

The following institutions and individuals helped me in the preparation of this book: the Historic O'Keefe Ranch, Vernon, BC; the Museum of the Cariboo Chilcotin, Williams Lake, BC; the Okanagan Archives Trust Society, Penticton, BC; the Royal BC Museum and BC Archives, Victoria, BC; Doug Cox; Mike Puhallo of the BC Cowboy Heritage Society, Kamloops, BC; Liz Twan; and my editor, Lesley Cameron.

INTRODUCTION

The Bunchgrass Ranges of British Columbia

In the silence that precedes sunrise a group of riders appeared over the hillside, silhouetted against the red glow of dawn. Below them in the shadows was a group of cattle, half-wild steers, wary of intruders after a summer in the cool upland ranges, untroubled by man. As soon as the riders appeared, the steers were up and off like deer, heading for the timber. With a whoop, the riders were after them, their horses straining. Across the grasslands the riders sped, forcing the cattle away from the timber and toward the lowlands. Before long the steers slowed to a lope and accepted their fate as the riders pulled up behind them and headed them through the bunchgrass range that stretched unfenced as far as the eye could see. It was roundup time in the British Columbia Interior.

Lying between the Coast Mountains and the mountain ranges culminating in the Rocky Mountains of British Columbia is a rugged upland area of valleys and high plateaus. The region's climate is largely influenced by the fact that it is separated from the Pacific coastal regions by a high range of mountains, creating a "rain shadow" effect where precipitation is lessened because warm moist air from the coast is dropped on the coastal mountains. The resulting hot, dry climate has meant that the plants and animals of the British Columbia Interior have had to adapt to a lack of moisture. They are accustomed to living where drought is common, summers are long and hot, and winters are cold and relatively dry. Of particular interest are the extensive grasslands, open areas where grasses or grass-like plants are the dominant vegetation and where there are few trees. Grasses dominate because they are better able to thrive in hot, dry climates where rain is sparse in spring and summer. They can also withstand grazing and fire. The growing point of

Bluebunch wheatgrass (*Pseudoroegnaria spicata*) is found in the driest soil-moisture regimes and lowest elevations of the BC Interior. *Ken Mather photo*

most plants is situated at the tip of a leaf or shoot, but in grasses it is at the base, close to the ground. When a grass plant has been grazed or burned it can grow again from this protected base.

The vast majority of grasslands in the British Columbia Interior are a type called bunchgrass. The term "bunchgrass" refers to types of grasses that grow in tufts or bunches from a single root system. As the stems of bunchgrasses grow up and outward from a narrow base, they form an "umbrella" that protects the base and root system from sun and evaporation. In a similar manner, the stems act as a funnel to channel moisture into the centre and down into the root system. Because of these characteristics, bunchgrasses are particularly well adapted to the very dry conditions found in the valleys and high plateaus west of the Coast Mountains. Three main types of bunchgrass are found in the BC Interior: bluebunch wheatgrass, rough fescue and Idaho fescue. Each is adapted to a specific soil-moisture regime and found at different altitudes and locations.

The grasslands of the British Columbia Interior remained undisturbed for thousands of years, the home of the Native people who lived a precarious existence as they struggled to amass enough food to survive through the often severe winters. They hunted for the game that could be found in their territory, especially the large animals that would occasionally come to graze on the rich bunchgrass. To supplement their diet they dug for nutritious roots that could be dried and pounded into a fine powder like flour for cakes. They also fished for the salmon that travelled up the main rivers in the Interior, dried them and preserved them for future use. Although it was a difficult life, they lived in a unity with their natural surroundings that made their simple lives fulfilling. But larger forces in the world were about to change their lives and cultures forever.

By the mid-1700s the Native groups in the interior of what is now British Columbia had horses. Seldom has the introduction of any animal so significantly changed the culture of a people as the horse did for the Native people of North America. Their semi-nomadic life, which involved carrying everything on their backs or on dogs and walking to the next food source, was changed forever by the horse. They could now travel great distances on horseback and, perhaps more significantly, they could transport greater amounts of food and material goods. By the time the early fur traders arrived in New Caledonia, as the interior of British Columbia was then known, the horse was already a significant part of Native culture and had become a symbol of wealth. The Natives of the Interior Plateau of British Columbia were the first stock raisers and over the years learned the advantage of good pasturage and water for the health of their animals.

Although the fur traders of the Hudson's Bay Company had brought cattle into the Interior as early as 1831, the first extensive importation of cattle into the area was during the gold rush years of 1858–1868. During that time, more than 22,000 head of cattle were brought into the new Crown colony of British Columbia to feed the thousands of miners. Some of these cattle became the foundation herds of the British Columbia cattle industry. They grazed on the lush bunchgrass ranges that could be found everywhere in the Interior. The cattle flourished and, by the turn of the century, the cattle industry had expanded to occupy most of the easily accessible bunchgrass ranges.

The 20th century was a time of incredible growth in ranching in British Columbia as the number of cattle grazing on the grasslands of the Interior increased exponentially. Even after the open bunchgrass ranges were occupied, enterprising and industrious pioneers sought out available land on the fringes of settlements. As late as the 1930s, adventurous individuals were still seeking out and finding new areas to graze cattle.

In many ways, the first half of the 20th century was the heyday of ranching in the province. The image of the cowboy had captured the imagination of the public. Rodeos were held in every town and city with any claim to ranching and the fledgling moving-picture industry glamorized the cowboy. By the 1930s, groups like the Sons of the Pioneers and movie cowboys like Gene Autry and Roy Rogers had made the image of the "singing cowboy" a part of the cowboy myth. As the mystique of the cowboy grew, thousands of young men and women became attracted to the ranching way of life.

The British were at the forefront of those who flocked to the Interior ranches. Coming from a society where the horse had been considered a status symbol for centuries, young British men and women were attracted to the cowboy life. But it was not only those who wanted to find a way out of the poverty and urban squalor of life in the cities of Britain who came. The best British families sent their younger sons to learn the ranching way of life and it was not unusual to hear a cultured Oxford accent around the campfire at night.

Ranching life was a great equalizer. The best educated and high-born mixed freely with the uneducated and uncultured. The only hierarchy in cowboying was based on achievement. Those who had been born to humble circumstances had every opportunity to rise to be cow boss or even ranch owner if they worked hard and had a gift for handling cattle. The Native people were particularly suited to the lifestyle and were treated as equals and accepted for their abilities from the beginning of the ranching era. Although Natives were often at a disadvantage, being unable to own their own land, they excelled as cowboys and often rose to positions of responsibility.

Bunchgrass range near Lundbom Lake in the Merritt area of the Nicola Valley. Bunchgrass areas interspersed with coniferous forest and small lakes are found throughout the Interior Plateau.
Ken Mather photo

Even the Chinese, who were discriminated against even more than the Native people were, found acceptance and employment on ranches.

The same could be said for gender differences. Women, especially those who had grown up on ranches, took their place alongside the men and contributed in many ways to the success of ranches. If they could ride and rope, they were welcome at the roundups, cattle drives, brandings and rodeos that were part of ranch life. Feminine qualities were held in great esteem by the rough cowboys and women were treated with respect and sometimes awe in a society where men outnumbered women two to one.

But those who came from around the world to be cowboys found that the romantic image of the cowboy bore only a slight resemblance to the realities of ranch life. Ranching involved long days in the saddle in the harshest of conditions, back-breaking work wrestling calves at the branding fire or putting up hay, feeding cattle in 40-below-zero weather, or breathing in the choking dust stirred up by hundreds of hooves during cattle drives. These were just some of the hardships that had to be endured. Illness and accidents were not uncommon in this rough life but, on some of the ranches, it was hundreds of miles over rough roads to the nearest doctor or hospital. Only the strongest were capable of withstanding the rugged lifestyle and demands that the climate and terrain imposed. The romance soon paled next to the grim reality of ranch life. And yet, there was the breathtaking scenery of the Interior, the incredible red glow of the sunrise over the mountains and, above all, the quiet of the vast rangelands, punctuated only by the soft rustle of grasses in the wind and the distant call of the coyote. For many, this life close to nature and away from the busy cities was just what they wanted. They were prepared to endure the hardships and pain for the joy of a life free from the constraints of civilization and at one with the Maker.

At a time when city dwellers had become jaded and cynical about their fellow man, the ranching community continued to practise the code of "Help your neighbour." If a member of the community was in need, neighbours would not hesitate to help out, even if it meant hardship for themselves. Barn and house raisings were common and, if a husband was injured or sick, neighbours would help with chores until he recovered. In the hard, sometimes dreary, life that ranchers on isolated homesteads lived, any opportunity to get together with neighbours was enthusiastically looked forward to. The entire community would gather together and pool resources for roundup, branding and other essential ranch activities. Settlers from the remote ranches would not hesitate to drive for days by horse and wagon to attend the annual race meets or occasional dances held in the one-room schoolhouses or halls.

In the ranching community, a man's word was his bond, and deals for thousands of dollars were confirmed by a handshake. A reputation for honesty and integrity was considered more valuable than any amount of cash. When credit was extended by the storekeepers or suppliers, every effort was made to live up to the commitment, even if it meant going without. These values were the foundation of the ranching community and, when the packing houses based in Vancouver saw only increased profits as their goal, the ranchers were slow to understand that they were being taken advantage of. They were equally slow to realize the strength of the cattle industry and organize themselves against the companies. Even when co-operatives were formed to try and achieve fairness, the fiercely independent ranchers were uncomfortable about having to organize.

Despite the demands of keeping a ranch operating smoothly, homesteaders and cowboys did not hesitate to enlist and serve in the two great wars that defined the first half of the 20th century. A disproportionate number of young men, especially Natives, from the ranching areas of the province joined the armed forces and served their country during the conflicts. Many of them did not return and often homesteads were left to become overgrown when their owners made the ultimate sacrifice. Countless others returned home physically or emotionally scarred. But there was nothing like the ranching way of life to bring a returning serviceman back to the lifestyle he knew before the war.

As if the world wars were not hardship enough, the years of the Great Depression took their toll on the ranching community as well. Prices for cattle plummeted and ranchers were barely able to cover their costs of living, let alone the maintenance of their cattle or horse herds and ranch infrastructure. Foreclosures and abandoned homesteads were the order of the day as cash became increasingly limited. But, for those who persevered, the postwar boom made ranching profitable again . . . until the next crisis.

Those who lived through these difficult times and endured the hardships and deprivation would later say that they wouldn't change it for the world. A life spent close to nature and where time clocks and narrow streets were unheard of was reward enough. No amount of money or luxury could take away from the freedom and joy of life as a cowboy or rancher.

Chapter One

The Great War

Cowboy Soldiers

Wee Tan Louie rode up to the bunkhouse at the Douglas Lake Ranch cow camp. He could hear loud voices from inside and noticed that Frank O'Keefe's horse was in the corral, meaning that he had ridden up from the home ranch. "I wonder what's new in the outside world," thought Wee Tan as he dismounted and unsaddled his horse before turning it loose in the corral. Wee Tan was one of the few Chinese cowboys on the Douglas Lake Ranch. The son of Chew Je Nuey (whose last name had been corrupted into "Louie"), who had come to British Columbia in 1858 during the height of the Cariboo gold rush, he had grown up at the Sullivan Ranch near Chase. Along with the rest of the children in the area, he had been educated at the Shuswap Prairie School, built by Whitfield Chase on his ranch. He had walked all the way to the Douglas Lake Ranch when he was 14 years old and found employment helping to dig irrigation ditches for the vast hayfields that the ranch was planting. Three years later, he was working as a cowboy from early spring to late fall.

Wee Tan entered the bunkhouse where the men were all talking at once. Frank O'Keefe had brought news that war had broken out in Europe and that Canada had entered the war. Most of the men were eager to enlist and go fight for their country and Wee Tan was no different. He was born and raised in British Columbia, spoke and wrote excellent English and was a rugged individual and accomplished horseman. But when he mentioned his desire to enlist, a silence descended on the room. "I don't think they'll be accepting any Chinamen," said one of the boys. "This is British Columbia and they don't have

Billy Brewer (left) and Johnny Harris, Okanagan cowboy soldiers. On the Okanagan's Head of the Lake Reserve, every eligible man enlisted. Johnny Harris was killed in the Battle of Amiens.
Historic O'Keefe Ranch photo

any use for the Chinese." Even the Native cowboys, who knew discrimination first-hand, nodded in agreement. Wee Tan was shocked. He had never thought of himself as being any different from the rest of the workers at the ranch. But he had to admit that things were getting worse for the Chinese. As soon as the Canadian Pacific Railway (CPR) had been completed, the federal government moved to restrict the immigration of Chinese to Canada. The first federal anti-Chinese bill was passed in 1885. It took the form of a head tax of $50 imposed, with few exceptions, upon every person of Chinese origin entering the country. The head tax was increased to $100 in 1900 and to $500 in 1903; $500 was equivalent to two years' wages for a Chinese labourer at that time. Meanwhile, Chinese were denied Canadian citizenship.

Nonetheless, Wee Tan rode to Kamloops and went to the enlistment office. But he was refused. "Orientals" were not allowed to enlist, as they were not considered citizens. Wee Tan tried several times but was consistently turned down. However, other provinces were more open to Chinese enlistment. By the fall of 1917 he had saved enough to purchase a horse and supplies and set out to Calgary to try his luck there. The journey took three months and, as winter closed in, the going was particularly rough, with freezing temperatures and blizzards. But he persevered and reached Calgary by February. Wanting to be sure this time, Wee Tan gave his name as William Thomas, a name he had spotted on a mailbox and, on February 20, 1918, he was accepted into the 10th Canadian Infantry Battalion. "William Thomas" Louie arrived in Bamshot, England, in April and, after basic training, crossed the Channel into the war zone. Because he was so quick on his feet, he served as a runner and, over the next seven months, served in France, the Netherlands and Belgium. Wee Tan returned to Canada in March 1919 and was honourably discharged after receiving the British War Medal and the Victoria Medal. Sadly, upon his return to British Columbia, his status had not changed. He was still not allowed to purchase land or to vote in elections. Wee Tan would have to wait until 1947 to be allowed to vote in the country for which he had fought and risked his life.

Not all young men in the British Columbia ranching community had the same difficulty in enlisting. In fact, young men from the Native reserves of BC enlisted in disproportionate numbers. On the Head of the Lake Okanagan Reserve, every eligible male between the ages of 20 and 35 enlisted. By 1916, Kamloops and the surrounding countryside had 4,000 men in arms. Shortly after the outbreak of the war, the Kamloops polo grounds became a mobilization centre and the army camp at Vernon, where the British Columbia Horse had trained in 1912 and 1913, was expanded to accommodate the flood of enlistments from the ranches and orchards of the Interior.

As soon as Canada declared war on Germany, two days after Germany invaded neutral Belgium, Prime Minister Borden offered to send an expeditionary force overseas to assist Britain. Sir Sam Hughes, minister of militia and defence, called for 25,000 volunteers but 33,000 enthusiastic young Canadian men enlisted within a month. The first contingent travelled overseas in 1914 and included two battalions formed almost entirely of 3,411 British Columbians. The 7th Battalion contained elements from the Duke of Connaught's Own Rifles, the 11th Fusiliers from Victoria, the Rocky Mountain Rangers (based in Kamloops in the heart of ranching country), the Westminster Fusiliers and the West Kootenay detachment. Half of the 16th (Canadian Scottish) Battalion came from the Seaforth Highlanders, based in Vancouver, and another quarter from the Gordon Highlanders of Victoria. Both these battalions served with the 1st Canadian Infantry Division of the Canadian Expeditionary Force. Another BC-based regiment was the 2nd Canadian Mounted Rifles, organized in December 1914. The regiment was mobilized at Willows Camp, Victoria, and recruited from British Columbia Horse (Vernon) and Victoria Squadron of Horse. The battalion went overseas in 1915 and served in France and Flanders with the 1st Canadian Mounted Rifle Brigade from September 1915 until January 1916, when it was reorganized and redesignated the 2nd Canadian Mounted Rifle Battalion of the 8th Infantry Brigade.

The group of seven cowboys who travelled from the Big Bar, Dog Creek and Gang Ranch areas of the Interior to enlist with the 158th Duke of Connaught's Own Rifles in Vancouver in January 1917 was typical. John Bunnage, Harold Willsher and Harry Marriott had been born in England, while Eddie and Alec Haller, Johnny Hartman and Sam Kersey were born in the BC Interior. Interestingly enough, all but Kersey listed their occupation as "Rancher." "Cowboy" was probably not an acceptable occupation name. All sailed for England from Halifax on November 14, 1916. They were stationed at Shoreham, England, until December 28, 1916, when they were sent to France for training at the Canadian Base in Étaples, France. Johnny Hartman was killed in action at the Battle of Amiens in August 1918, at the age of 21 years. The largely Canadian effort resulted in an advance of just under 12 miles into German-held territory. Later, German General Ludendorff described the Battle of Amiens as "the black day of the German Army in the history of this war." Johnny paid the ultimate price but all six of his buddies returned to Canada after the war.

The ranching country of the British Columbia Interior soon emptied of young men as hundreds went to enlist, and the ranches began to resemble a home for the very old and very young. Even some of the younger men made an effort to join the war effort. Albert Nichol, whose father had taken up land at Long Lake south of Kamloops, got all the way to Halifax before it was discovered that he was only 14. He was sent home but succeeded in enlisting in the Second World War. Because of the scarcity of labour, wages were higher for those who were available, affecting the profit margin on beef. But the downturn in profits was soon offset by soaring prices. The price per head of cattle increased from $80 in 1914 to $111.43 in 1919.

For the hundreds of German-speaking people in the ranching country of British Columbia, the outbreak of the war caused mixed feelings. They were torn between love for their mother country and loyalty to their adopted country and were confused about how to respond. Andrew Manning was working on a haying crew near Kamloops for a German rancher when war broke out. The rancher sat the haying crew down to explain that his homeland and Canada were now at war and the crew was free to go. All the men, recognizing that their country was not at war with this good man who just happened to be from Germany, agreed to stay until the haying was done. Manning also tells the story of one of his neighbours receiving his call-up papers from the army, just like hundreds of other reservists in the Interior. The only difference was that his neighbour had been called up by Kaiser Wilhelm and the papers were in German, mailed from Berlin. Needless to say, the papers were quickly filed in the woodstove.

Supplying the War Effort

British Columbia supplied much more than men for the war effort. As the war was being fought at a time when motorized vehicles were in their infancy, horses were still considered an essential form of locomotion. They were widely used in the first years of the war, both for mounted cavalry units and for hauling heavy guns and equipment to the front. The British, French and Canadian armies all had purchasing agents in Canada who scoured the country looking for cavalry remounts and artillery horses. As the British Columbia Interior had many wild horses, quite a market developed for those cowboys who could catch, break and train horses. All the army required was for a horse to be ridden two or three times to be considered gentle enough for the troops. Returning soldiers were heard to remark, "Those damned remounts killed or wounded more men than did the German army."

John Roper Hull's Edith Lake Ranch, south of Kamloops, supplied many horses to the military. The same applied to Joe Bulman's Willow Ranch, which became a centre for breaking and training remounts. Given the shortage of good manpower, a man who was tough enough to break horses day in and day out was worth a lot. One of these men was Bill Arnold, who arrived in the Nicola Valley from Montana with his father, also named Bill, early in the war. Arnold Sr. (Old Bill) was a big, barrel-chested man who had worked with horses since he was a youngster. Young Bill was about 44 years old when he arrived but soon gained a reputation as a man who could ride "anything that wore hide." He went to work at the Willow Ranch, halter-breaking and "sacking out" the wild horses that had been captured in the nearby hill country. He then turned them over to several young "bronc twisters" who did most of the riding. If they ran into a real tough horse, Bill would hop on and ride it to a standstill.

In the area south of Kamloops, there were quite a few locally famous bucking horses. One of them was particularly mean and had the bad habit of rearing up and falling over backwards, trapping the rider beneath several hundred pounds of horse with the saddle horn or cantle right in the rider's chest or stomach. The owner of the horse bet $100 to any takers that the horse could not be ridden. Bill Arnold, always up for the challenge, took him up on the bet.

Once word got around that Bill was going to ride the beast, quite a crowd assembled to watch the fun. The horse was saddled and the cinch pulled up tight and, true to form, the horse humped its back and puffed up like a bullfrog. Before he got into the saddle, Bill took his heavy, shot-loaded quirt by the lash end and, as he hit the saddle, swung the quirt down as hard as he could between the horse's ears. The horse, stunned by the blow, dropped to its knees and then jumped up and took off at a dead run without as much as a buck. After a mad dash to the end of the pasture, Bill managed to bring him to a halt, then turned him and ran him back to the waiting crowd. By then the horse was tired out and slowed to a walk. Bill grinned and said, "Seems like he forgot to buck." Then he collected his $100 and headed home.

Bill's father, Old Bill, had a cabin at Lac du Bois, north of Kamloops, that he used as a base for prospecting the surrounding mountains. Old Bill was a unique character and had his own cures for the ailments that afflicted him from time to time. Alex Bulman tells the story of his dad, Joe, riding by Old Bill's cabin one hot summer day and thinking he would stop in for a drink of cool water and a visit. When he got off his horse and knocked at the cabin door, Old Bill appeared, naked as the day he was born. Not only that, but his body was smeared with a mixture of beef tallow and brown sugar. Bill was delighted to have a visitor and invited him in. But the interior of the cabin was like a sauna, with the woodstove going full blast. Old Bill proudly announced that the combination of heat and the mixture of tallow and sugar was just the cure for the rheumatism that had been bothering him. Needless to say, Joe Bulman didn't stay for long.

Old Bill displayed another interesting trait on his occasional visits to Kamloops for supplies. Once he had done his shopping, he would buy a bottle of the strongest rum. With that in his pocket, he would visit Burns Meat Market and purchase a beefsteak that he would proceed to eat raw, much to the surprise of anyone who happened to be in the store. Then he would take a long swig of the rum, saying "That will cook the steak in my stomach." Say what you will about Old Bill's eccentric habits, he lived to the ripe old age of 90.[1]

Another man who made much of the demand for horses during the war was Gussie Haller, son of Joe Haller, one of the original settlers in the Big Bar area. In those days there were hundreds of wild horses on the open ranges around Big Bar Creek that ran into the Fraser River. Haller would go out in the spring when the wild horses were at their weakest, having scratched for feed through the snow all winter. In the early spring while there was still snow on the ground, he would ride a big, healthy, grain-fed horse and simply outrun the wild horses, roping them and breaking them to lead right on the range. As the wild horses grew healthier on the rich bunchgrass ranges of the

Wild horse corral west of 100 Mile House. The corrals had to be up to 10 feet high to contain the wild horses. *Historic O'Keefe Ranch photo*

area, he had to develop a different strategy. He would build a stout corral, up to 10 feet high, out of Jack pine logs, with log wings 200–300 yards long fanning out from the entrance to the corral. Gussie most often worked by himself, sometimes driving the wild horses for miles until they could be funnelled into the corral. It took nerve and a fine horse to drive a bunch of wild horses through the brush and timber, so bruises and scrapes would be guaranteed. Once he had them headed into the corral, he would have to be right at the tail end of the herd of wild horses to close the gate to the corral, as the horses would turn on a dime and head out once they realized they were trapped. The corral would always be round, as a wild horse could make short work of a man if he was trapped in a corner. Gussie would rope and snub the horse up to a post in the corral so he could saddle and break it. The wild horses could be trained into tough, hardy saddle or pulling horses but had to be kept confined or catching them to harness would be a daunting proposition. Their wild horse instincts were never fully quashed.

Bronc Busting

The job of transforming a wild horse fresh off the range into a gentle, responsive horse that could be used as a partner with the rider in any task required of it was the role of the bronc buster, also known as the bronc twister, bronc peeler or rough string rider. The term "bronc" comes from the Spanish *bronco*, meaning "wild," and appropriately names the horse in its natural state in the wild. While the terms "breaking," "twisting" and "peeling" all suggest a battle of wills in which the human is ultimately the winner, the actual process of training a horse for work is more appropriately called "gentling." By the early 1900s, the heavy-handed methods of "choking a horse down," saddling it and climbing on to ride it while applying the spurs and quirt were pretty much gone. Ranchers wanted horses with spirit and any man who abused horses did not last too long as a bronc buster. Busters took great pride in their work and did their best to make good horses and not spoil them. Over the years, techniques were developed to gentle the horse without damaging the spirit or the body of the animal. Obviously, if a bronc buster was paid to turn out "green broke" horses for resale, he would use quicker and rougher methods. However, even though there were many variations on the process of breaking a horse, the basics were the same throughout North America's ranching country.

An outsider may well ask, "What constitutes a broken horse?" The bronc buster and the owner of the horse wanted to end up with a horse that had been taught to stand while being handled and to respond to the rein of the rider. A horse also had to learn to lead, referred to as being "halter broke." Finally, the rider had to be able to control the horse so it would not buck while being worked. This is not to say that a good horse might not buck a bit to "get the kinks out" when first saddled and ridden in the morning.

A horse was considered to be of breaking age when it was between three and a half and four years old. Having lived in a wild state on the range for all its life, the horse was usually strong, wild and hard to ride. The horse would be driven into a round pen to be worked for the first time. In British Columbia, where timber was never too far away from the ranch headquarters, the pen would be made of good-sized timbers. The round pen was designed especially for catching and handling horses. It placed the roper within easy throwing distance of the horse and prevented the horse from getting a straight run away from the roper, always being pushed in toward him by the curve of the pen. It was also important to keep a horse moving in a round pen, so that the bronc buster could rope it. As well, once the horse was caught and saddled, the round pen made it easier for the rider to turn it and keep it going.

There were two methods of roping a horse in the round pen. The first was to throw the loop over its head and "choke it down" or snub it to a post. This technique was more apt to injure the horse and made it much more nervous when first approached by a man. The other method was to rope the horse by its forefeet, called "forefooting." In most cases, the horse would be thrown down once it was forefooted but, if a bronc buster was working alone, he could leave the horse standing. Either way, once the horse was caught, the bronc buster would slowly tighten up the rope until the horse's forefeet were tight together. Usually the bronc buster had a helper, called a "hazer," for the initial stages of breaking. When the horse was down, the hazer would sit on the horse's neck and slip on a hackamore, a term that comes from Spanish, like so many in ranching. *Jaquima* means "halter" or "headstall." The hackamore, instead of using

A bronc buster (on the right) and his "hazer" preparing to rope a horse for breaking. The horses have been fed some hay to distract them so they can be easily roped.
Okanagan Heritage Museum photo

a bit in the horse's mouth, had a noseband, called a bosel, which worked by putting pressure on the horse's nose. For particularly wild horses, one of the horse's back legs would be tied up with a rope around the horse's neck to make it even more manageable. Some bronc busters liked to put a blindfold on the horse that could be lifted when the rider was ready to mount. Once the horse was prepared in this way, it was allowed to stand up and the actual job of breaking could begin.

The first lesson that the horse learned was to get used to things touching it, a process called "sacking out." A grain sack was generally used but a saddle blanket or even a canvas tarp had the same result. The sack was held out in front of the horse's head so that it could smell the sack and realize it was harmless. The sack would then be gently rubbed over the horse's nose and head. It was important to rub it over the horse's eyes as this caused the horse to close its eyes and relax. All this time the bronc buster would be talking gently to the horse to calm it and convince it that he was not a threat. Then the sack was rubbed over the horse's neck and then around its legs and underneath the body so that every part of the horse's anatomy was touched. Eventually the bronc buster would be able to flap the sack to get the

horse used to sounds around and behind it. Many bronc busters took this opportunity to trim the horse's tail and the mane hair that extended along the withers. This allowed horses that had been broken to stand out in a herd for ease of identification.

When the horse was well sacked and convinced that it was not under any serious threat, the sack was placed over its neck and a saddle blanket placed over its back. Standing to the front of the horse, the bronc buster would then gently place the saddle on the horse's back. The cinch would be drawn under the horse, sometimes with a hooked stick, and pulled up to be attached to the latigo strap. The cinch would gradually be tightened but, as the horse was usually holding its breath, the bronc buster would have to make sure that it let its breath out so the cinch would be secure. Many bronc busters would give the horse a knee in the ribs to make it let its breath out but some would also take the time to watch the horse's breathing and tighten the cinch when the breath was going out. The horse would finally be ready to ride for the first time.

It was always a good idea to let the horse get used to the saddle before jumping on. Some bronc busters would place their foot in the stirrup and put pressure on the saddle a few times before mounting. It was always important to place just the ball of the foot in the stirrup because, if the foot was fully into the stirrup and the horse whirled or jumped, the rider could be caught up and dragged off. Then the rider would swing up into the saddle. This was when the real fun would begin. Even the gentlest horse would buck, or as it was termed, "come apart," "blow up" or "unwind." The bronc buster's job was to stay on board and try to keep the horse's head up, as this made it more difficult for it to buck. If the breaking was being done in the round pen, the top rail, called the "opry house," was often full of spectators at this point.

This is where the bronc buster would earn his keep. He needed to know every trick there was to stay on the horse, and if he was bucked off, as was often the case, he needed to know how to land. He would kick his feet clear of the stirrups, go limp and roll on the ground. And then he had to get right back on, as the horse must not think that it had won the battle. The first ride was always the worst and generally three "saddles" (rides), happening on three successive days, were considered enough to call the horse "green broke." During those three rides, a good bronc buster would be able to teach the horse to respond to the reins and turn on command. The horse would also learn to respond to the pull of the lead rope (usually a braided horsehair rope called a *mecate*) on the halter. For the third "saddle," the horse would be taken outside the corral to be turned in either direction and to be ridden alternately at a walk, trot and gallop. Once this three-day process was complete, the horse was considered broken.

Each of the three "saddles" would take about an hour, so a good bronc buster could work as many as 8 or 10 horses in a single day. Because of the incredibly rough and dangerous work involved, most bronc busters were no older than 30. They were considered the best cowboys around and looked upon with respect long after their productive years were over. Old-time cowboy Ramon Adams summed them up well. "Ridin' a buckin' hoss, if not an art, was shore a contest requirin' skill, courage, and strength, especially if it happened to be a hoss that was spoiled or had acquired a bad habit from general cussedness. I doubt if there was any one thing in connection with ranch work or a rodeo performance that was more excitin' than a good rider on a good buckin' hoss." [2]

Community Life

Although there was a move toward the consolidation of ranch properties into large ranches, the smaller family-operated ranch was still the norm in British Columbia. An abiding sense of community and the value of neighbours were important for people whose lives were far from easy. There was seldom any hesitation about helping out a neighbour and those who refused to acknowledge the importance of co-operation and community did not last long. Every community had its gathering point, usually where the first post office had been established, and there were occasional opportunities for the entire community to gather for social events. In a time when the drudgery of ranch work left little time for relaxation, these were opportunities for people to get up to date on each other's lives and for young people to look for possible spouses.

Roadhouses

The gathering place for the Riske Creek area of the Chilcotin was unquestionably Becher's store. Fred Becher (pronounced "Beecher"), a big, good-looking man, had become postmaster of the Chilcoten (as it was spelled in those days) Post Office in 1894 and remained so for the next 30 years. His store, hotel and saloon, admirably situated on a long expanse of winding dirt road, soon earned a reputation as the best stopping house in the Chilcotin. The store was very well stocked and Becher was generous in letting ranchers run a line of credit until they sold their cattle in the fall. Becher was also eager to embrace the new technology that was changing the outside world. In 1912, a telephone line was strung through the Chilcotin and the first phone in the area was installed in his hotel. The following year, Becher brought a Cadillac motor car into the country, just about the time Jack Temple was bringing one into the nearby Hanceville area. He hired Ira J. Purkeypile to drive the car and ran a taxi service between Hanceville and 150 Mile House. The highlight of the year for many Chilcotinites was the annual week-long race meet held on Becher's Prairie. Becher was doing very well by the time the First World War started, with 200 head of cattle, a flock of sheep and a herd of horses. In addition, he owned several excellent hay meadows. But disaster struck in 1915, when his main building, which housed the hotel, store and saloon, burned to the ground. However, ever positive, Becher embarked on the construction of a new, even grander building using lumber from his own water-driven sawmill. The new stopping house had 22 rooms with a private sitting room for women travellers and a "smoking room" for the men.[3]

Becher married Florence Cole, the daughter of an English clergyman, in 1917 and brought her to the new Becher House. The couple lived a life of luxury for a time, with the new Mrs. Becher entertaining visitors over a lace tablecloth and fine silver tea service. Dances at the house were elegant affairs and the annual Becher Ball brought people in from as far away as Soda Creek and 150 Mile House. Guests stayed in the hotel or camped in the yard. Unfortunately for Fred Becher, the financial strain of rebuilding coupled with the growing use of the automobile for travel and the coming of Prohibition

Race meet at Becher's Prairie in the Chilcotin. The highlight of the year for many Chilcotinites was this annual week-long event. *Museum of the Cariboo Chilcotin, Williams Lake photo*

meant that business declined and debt piled up. When he died in 1935, his finances were a disaster.

In the Lac la Hache area, the community gathered at the 115 Mile House, owned since the gold rush days by the McKinleys. For hundreds of years, the Native community had gathered at the lake for games and socializing. Competitions would include foot races, wrestling, a traditional Native stick game and, of course, horse racing. Archibald McKinley constructed a racetrack on part of his ranch and, with his brother-in-law, Isaac Ogden, began raising racehorses. Races were held all week long and horses from Alkali Lake, Clinton, Ashcroft, Kamloops and Merritt competed, with the McKinley horses taking away a substantial portion of the prizes. The gathering always included a dance. One of the stagecoach drivers, Arthur Haddock, described the scene: "Following the races, and for many years, a dance, which usually lasted all week, took place at the 115 Mile House. In later years they were held in a community hall built across the road from the roadhouse. The crowd broke into three groups, so that at any one time there was always a group sleeping, another eating, and a third one dancing. The celebration would have lasted even longer, if the 45 gallon keg of 'Scotland's Finest' had held out."[4]

The McKinley roadhouse dining room also served the community as a host of the weekly church service and, during the war years, the McKinleys hosted dances, card parties and whist parties as Red Cross fundraisers. The roadhouse also served as a base for other social gatherings, including school picnics and meetings of the Art Club and Farmers' Institute.

Further north, the 150 Mile House served as the social centre. Since the gold rush days, it had been one of the major stops on the way to the goldfields and had prospered under various owners. By 1912, the house and surrounding land had been purchased by the Cariboo Trading Company. The company described the operation at that time: "The property . . . has been enlarged from 1500 acres to 4000 acres, with a cattle herd of 800 head, mostly shorthorn . . . Two large buildings, the hotel and store, supply all the needs of the local district. There are extensive store houses and stables, one of which has space for 66 horses, and lofts to hold 80 tons of hay. A good annual crop of garden produce supplies the needs of the store and hotel."[5]

Like most roadhouses in those days, it had no central heating, with all the heat being supplied from heaters on the main floor that had stovepipes which extended through the roof. This meant that the upstairs rooms could be extremely cold in the winter. During very cold weather, guests were brought a pre-breakfast hot toddy to help ignite the internal fires. Alvin Johnston of Quesnel stayed in the hotel on one particularly cold December night. Since the hotel was quite full, he was given a small room at the very back of the upstairs. Despite consuming numerous hot rums before retiring, Johnston spent a long night huddled in his bed trying to stay warm. When morning finally arrived, he rushed downstairs to warm up beside the main heater. A few minutes earlier, an early-morning traveller had arrived at the hotel, completely swaddled in outdoor clothing and with long icicles hanging from his moustache. As he stood beside the stove, Johnston took one look at him and asked, "My God, which room did you have?"[6]

Many of the roadhouses in the British Columbia Interior were eventually destroyed by fire, often caused by faulty chimneys or overturned oil lamps, and the 150 Mile House was no exception. It burned to the ground in the early morning of February 13, 1916. Fortunately there was no loss of life, but there was one near tragedy. Alex Meiss of Horsefly had to flee his room without his most prized possession: his wooden leg. While being carried to safety by the hotel manager, Alex shouted that his wooden leg was still in the burning building. Spurred by Alex's cries, an intrepid hero rushed into the building and through the smoke and flames and successfully rescued the leg. The Cariboo Trading Company did not rebuild the hotel but continued to operate the store until 1928.

Roundup and Branding

A significant event in the social life of any ranching community was the fall round-up. In ranching areas like the Chilcotin, where many small ranchers ran their cattle on common grazing grounds, these events were attended by the whole family. Most of the ranchers from Redstone to Big Creek ranged their cattle together on the open bunchgrass prairie south of the Chilcotin River, and

Dr. Bruce McEwan and May Smithers at a South Okanagan roundup. It was not uncommon to see a woman riding sidesaddle at Interior roundups. *Okanagan Archives Trust photo, courtesy of Doug Cox, Myers Collection*

each family would bring a wagon loaded with enough food and bedding to last for a couple of weeks. The roundup would take place during the day as cattle were rounded up from a specific range and brought to a central holding area. Women were directly involved in the activities and did not necessarily confine themselves to cooking. Many of the younger girls were as capable with a horse or rope as any of the men and would hold their own in the rough brush country and steep terrain. Interestingly, during the war years, some of the women still rode sidesaddle. It was a sight to behold to see a cowgirl racing down a steep grade after an uncooperative steer while riding sidesaddle. Some

of the women even broke horses using a sidesaddle. The evenings, after a hearty meal of beans, bannock and beef, were a time for singing, storytelling and fiddle-playing around the campfire. The English and Irish ranchers had separate branding corrals, and years later the two big pastures were still called the Englishman Corral Pasture and the Irishman Corral Pasture.

Branding time was another opportunity for the entire community to get together. In the Nicola Valley, late May and early June was branding time. All the ranchers who had cattle on the Hamilton Commonage would gather at the Douglas Lake Ranch's Hamilton corrals, southeast of the home ranch. Aside from the Douglas Lake ranchers, there would be representatives from the Guichon, Lauder, Abbott and Sellers ranches. Cowboys from each of the ranches worked together to round up over 4,000 head of cattle spread across 16,000 acres of the commonage. Each ranch would show up with a crew of cowboys and a chuckwagon crammed with food, dishes, tents, bedrolls, branding irons and much more. Sometimes a second wagon was needed to carry all the gear required for the job, which took weeks to accomplish. In addition, the ranches each brought a string of horses and they were turned loose in an enclosed area to graze for the night.

Joe Coutlee, who had been cow boss at the Douglas Lake Ranch since the late 1890s, had overall charge of the roundup. In the early hours of the morning, well before dawn, Coutlee would holler, in a voice certainly designed to wake the dead, for the wranglers who would mount the horses they had picketed for the night and head out in the dark to bring in the horses into four corrals. By then, a hearty breakfast of beefsteak, bacon, beans, bread and coffee would be ready. It would be served off the backs of the chuckwagons and the cowboys would eat in canvas tents by the light of coal-oil lamps. Then they would head out and find their horse among the 150 or so in the corral, throw a loop over its head, saddle it and mount, ready for the day's work.

Coutlee would divide the Hamilton Commonage into 10 or 12 wedge-shaped sections and send riders to the far end of a new section each morning to sweep the area, gradually driving the cattle into the centre where the mothers and calves would be matched up and pushed into corrals depending upon the mother's brand. Then, after a quick lunch, a 30-foot-long branding fire would be lit and the branding would begin. The calves would be heeled (roped by the back feet) and dragged to the branding fire where they would be wrestled down and stretched out by two cowboys, one at the head and one at the rear. A third cowboy would remove the appropriate branding iron from the fire and apply the brand while yet another cowboy castrated the calf if it was a bull calf and notched its ear. With several teams working at one time, the process was quick and efficient. When all the calves from one ranch were done, they were turned loose to join their mothers that had been bellowing for their babies the whole time. Once all the calves had been branded, the herd was driven back to the part of the commonage that it had come from that morning. Herds from the Lauder, Sellers and Abbott ranches were driven directly to their nearby summer range. At the end of the branding, toward the end of June, the remaining cattle were driven to their respective ranches and the Hamilton Commonage remained empty until the following spring. Joe Coutlee and his crew of cowboys would move the Douglas Lake and Guichon cattle in smaller droves of about 250 head until they met up with the Guichon crew, who would take them to the Courtenay Lake crossing. Then another Douglas Lake crew would take them and push them onto the summer range near Aspen Grove at the Portland cow camp. The Guichon and Douglas Lake ranches shared the summer range and another one near Kingvale. This arrangement continued until 1940.

When all the cattle were established on their summer ranges in mid-summer, Joe Coutlee would rise one morning and roar, "Today's Sunday!" Regardless of the day of the week, the cowboys, after seemingly endless seven-day weeks, would have some time off. Only a few cowboys would be needed to ride the summer range or to drive cattle to markets, so the rest

Roping a calf for branding at the Alkali Lake Ranch. The mounted cowboy has roped the calf's hind legs so that it can be dragged to the branding fire without injury. *Museum of the Cariboo Chilcotin, Williams Lake photo*

Branding at the Alkali Lake Ranch. Note the Native cowboys, who are wearing their hair long and braided. *Museum of the Cariboo Chilcotin, Williams Lake photo*

of them would be laid off or added to the haying crews. This midsummer slack time gave most of the cowboys an opportunity to gravitate to the bars at Quilchena or Merritt. The Quilchena bar, the closest "watering hole" to the big ranches, was always busy, but never more so than during the days around July 1 when horse races were held on the adjoining racetrack. The bar was operated by Joe Guichon Jr., who ruled it with an iron hand. Cowboys who became too exuberant were locked up in the hotel root cellar, a gloomy hole that had the desired sobering effect. The Prohibition Act of 1917 may have closed the bars in British Columbia's cattle country but it had failed to stop people drinking alcohol. Enforcement was difficult. Doctors could freely prescribe liquor, bootlegging flourished and alcohol could be imported from other provinces for personal use. In a 1920 plebiscite, voters abandoned Prohibition and approved a system of government control and sale of liquor. Prohibition was officially repealed in 1921—on the same day that government liquor stores opened.[7]

Hunting

Hunting was another way that members of the community would get together, but on a smaller scale. Deer were abundant in the bush country of the Interior and venison was a welcome change from a diet of beef for the ranch families. There were also caribou in the Chilcotin and Cariboo regions, but, surprisingly, moose were unheard of in the earliest days of ranching in those areas. For whatever reason, moose only began to be seen in the war years. The first moose was reported in the Riske Creek area in 1914 and was shot in the Harper meadow. This new animal was a complete puzzle for the Native people. A Tsilhqot'in man named Moleese shot a moose in the fall of 1916 but didn't quite know what to do with it, being unsure whether it was good to eat. He cut out the tongue and lips and took them to his friends to see if they could identify this strange animal. None of them had any idea, and even the band elders had never heard of such an animal. But they did decide that the meat was good to eat, so they cut it up and packed it back home. The mystery was solved by Fred Becher, who ran the store at Riske Creek and identified the animal when Moleese brought in the hide and horns. Becher had worked for the Hudson's Bay Company in the North and had seen many moose. By 1930, moose were plentiful in the Chilcotin and were a welcome source of meat.

A similar encounter took place in the Dog Creek area in 1923. Sam Sault John, a Shuswap man, shot a strange animal a short distance from the Dog Creek settlement. After examining the animal, he rode back to the little settlement and shouted for everyone to come and look at the strange creature. Everyone within earshot came to look and Charlie Place, who owned the D4 Ranch, took his team of horses along. The dead animal was lying in the creek but, as Charlie approached, the horses balked at the new smell and it took some time before he could hitch them to the beast and pull it out of the creek. At first, everyone thought it was a horse but then they saw the horns. After some discussion, Charlie's wife, Ada, who was quite well read, stepped forward and declared, "It's a moose." She had seen pictures of them in books. Although reluctant to take her word for it, the locals had to admit it seemed likely she was correct. Eventually she was vindicated when she was able to point out pictures in her encyclopedia. It didn't take long for everyone to admit that the meat was good and, as the years went by, more and more moose were seen in the area.[8]

The Iron Horse

Since the completion of the CPR in 1885, ranchers in the Cariboo–Chilcotin had been driving their cattle on the long overland trek to Ashcroft where they would be loaded into stock cars and shipped to the coastal markets. For those in more isolated areas, the drive would take weeks and would result in the cattle losing weight, which would jeopardize their price when they arrived in Ashcroft. So, in 1912, when the provincial government announced that construction would begin on the Pacific Great Eastern Railway (PGE) from Squamish to Quesnel via Lillooet, there was great enthusiasm in the Interior. This railway was intended to eventually unite North Vancouver with the Grand Trunk Pacific Railway at Fort George, providing Cariboo–Chilcotin ranchers with easy access to the coastal markets. By 1914, Premier McBride was already talking about extending it to the Peace River and eventually to Alaska.

Unfortunately, the construction of the Pacific Great Eastern Railway was fraught with charges of corruption and poor management. By the time the track had been laid from Squamish to Clinton in 1917, the entire appropriation of $20 million had been spent. In early 1918, the railway's backers agreed to pay the government $1.1 million and turn the railway over to the government. By the early 1920s, the line had only been completed as far as Quesnel and no one could be found to buy the struggling railway. People joked that the PGE was the only railway that "started nowhere and finished nowhere." It did not connect with any other railway, and there were no large urban centres on its route. The unfortunate state of the railway caused it to be given nicknames such as "Province's Great Expense," "Prince George Eventually," "Past God's Endurance" and "Please Go Easy." Nonetheless, the line provided rail transportation for sending Cariboo–Chilcotin cattle to the lucrative coastal markets. Stock pens were constructed at regular intervals along the line—Lillooet, Pavilion, Kelly Lake, Clinton, Chasm (59 Mile), Lone Butte, Lac la Hache, Williams Lake, Alexandria and Quesnel—to serve the ranchers.

The only problem with the railway terminating at Squamish was that the cattle cars had to be loaded onto barges and pulled by tugboat down the coast to Vancouver. This resulted in seasickness among the cattle and long waits until the tide was favourable, much to the distress of both the cattlemen and the meat packers.

One of the most significant by-products of the Pacific Great Eastern Railway's construction was the establishment of Williams Lake as its divisional headquarters. Williams Lake had been located at the junction of the River Trail and the old Hudson's Bay Company Brigade Trail during the early gold rush years, and had become a thriving community. But Gustavus Blin Wright, the contractor for the construction of the Cariboo Wagon Road, had decided against the road passing through Williams Lake. Instead, it branched off from 150 Mile House to avoid the rough country north of Williams Lake, leaving the small community as a backwater. However,

50 years after it had been bypassed, Williams Lake was rejuvenated by being included on the proposed railway line. The provincial government purchased the "lower farm"[9] from Bob Borland in 1912 and established a new townsite for Williams Lake. After some deliberation as to whether the name of the new townsite should be Borland, the name Williams Lake was retained. The coming of the railway meant that the new town's population was swelled by trackmen, station agents and others and that it also became the main supply centre for the Cariboo–Chilcotin. Stockyards were constructed and, from that point on, Williams Lake became the destination for shipping cattle from all over the Cariboo–Chilcotin. After years of watching the traffic on the Cariboo Road bypass Williams Lake in favour of 150 Mile House, there was some justice in watching 150 Mile House become a quiet backwater.

As the PGE railway was making its slow progress through the Cariboo, another railway was being constructed through the southern part of the province. The Kootenays had been the site of a mining boom since the 1890s but had been so isolated from the rest of the province that the rich minerals had gone south on the US-owned railway, the Great Northern, which shipped them to markets. Similarly, supplies for the booming mining towns of the Kootenays had been coming north from the US. The Great Northern entered British Columbia at the town of Midway and crossed the border again at Bridesville, only to re-enter at Nighthawk in the Similkameen valley. From there, it went on to Keremeos and Princeton. The backers of the new railway intended to build a line that ran from the coast to the Kootenays so that the wealth would pass through British Columbia. At the same time, the rich cattle country of the South Okanagan and Similkameen would have access to rail service. So, at a time when railway schemes (and scandals) were many and varied, the fledgling Kettle Valley Railway Company and the great Canadian Pacific Railway reached an agreement to construct a branch line from Merritt in the Nicola Valley all the way to Midway in the Kootenays. From Merritt, the line would proceed south and follow the Coquihalla River to Hope to connect with the CPR main line.

Construction began in 1910 and, after painfully slow progress over incredibly rough terrain, the section from Midway to Merritt was completed in 1915. From there, construction proceeded through the Coquihalla Pass to Hope and the work was completed in 1916. Even though the Kettle Valley Railway was one of the most expensive railroads ever built and never managed to pay off its construction debt, it kept the wealth of the Kootenays in British Columbia and, almost as an aside, guaranteed that the rich bunchgrass ranges of the South Okanagan and Similkameen would remain cattle country with secure access to the coastal markets.

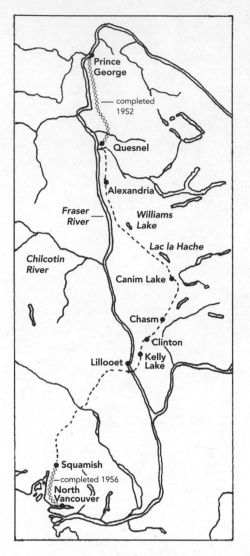

Pacific Great Eastern Railway Line

In most cases, the railways were a reliable means of getting cattle to market. But there were occasional disasters. In the fall of 1919, Hans Richter drove two carloads of cattle, 24 to a carload, from the Richter Estate Ranch to Penticton. The cattle were for the Swift Canadian Company in Vancouver and were loaded into the two cattle cars without any problem. As the train proceeded over the Coquihalla Pass, the two carloads were pulled onto a siding so the engine could be shunted onto a side track. Although the brakes were on, the movement of the cattle caused the cars to start rolling right down the main line. They got going so fast that both cars jumped the track and plunged down a cliff, breaking up the cars below. More than half the cattle were killed, or injured so badly that they had to be killed. But one black cow with a white face escaped the mess and climbed back up the cliff, obviously having seen enough of the disaster.

The railways did not only change how cattle were transported, they also brought about changes in how the cattle were treated. Their widespread use prompted a demand for de-horning. Almost all cattle in the early days had long, uplifted horns that they used as protection against predators in the wild. The horns also made it easier for a cowboy to rope a cow as they kept a rope from slipping off if it did not go around the whole head. But when it came time to loading cattle into a cattle car the horns were a real problem. Not

(preceding pages) Canadian Pacific Railway cattle car. The main CPR shipping locations in the BC Interior were Kamloops and Ashcroft. *Royal BC Museum, BC Archives photo I-30844*

only were the horns dangerous to cowboys working close to the cattle, but the horn tips would also puncture the hides of adjacent cattle in a crowded car. They also made it difficult to load more than 12 to 14 head into a car without overcrowding. Some ranches began to import polled breeds of cattle, like the Angus and Galloway, which were naturally without horns. But most ranchers were not impressed with these breeds and felt that they could neither put on weight nor defend themselves on the range as well as the Hereford and Shorthorn breeds. So the ranchers began the practice of de-horning. This process usually involved pushing the cattle into "squeezes" that restrained them so that large cutters could lop off the horns. This process was difficult and stressful for mature cattle, and involved some blood loss, so ranchers began "de-budding" calves when their horns were just beginning to show. This could be accomplished with minimum stress to the animal and rancher alike. The downside of de-horning, of course, was that the cattle were less able to defend themselves against predators on the open range but anywhere from 35 to 55 head of hornless cattle, depending upon size, could be put into a cattle car. As time progressed, more polled breeds of cattle, including polled Herefords, were developed.

The Horseless Carriage

By the time the First World War broke out, the transition from the horse-drawn wagon to the motor car was well underway. The first automobile arrived in the Cariboo in 1907 when O.P. Perry of the Bullion Mine near Likely drove his McLaughlin Buick up the Cariboo Road. Thinking that this newfangled "horseless buggy" was the transportation of the future, a group of Cariboo citizens formed the Cariboo Automobile Company with the intention of driving a regular run from Ashcroft to Soda Creek. But the 40-horsepower Rambler broke down on its first trip and never ran again.

The BC Express Company (BX), which had run stagecoaches on the Cariboo Road since the gold rush days, watched this new venture with interest and, in 1910, sent Willis West to Vancouver and Seattle to check out the selection of automobiles. The first vehicle he looked at was a 17-passenger touring car built by the Russell Car Company of Vancouver. When he asked to take it for a test run, he was told that he couldn't because it was raining outside. Deciding that a car that couldn't be taken out in the rain wouldn't last very long in the Cariboo, West moved on. In Seattle, he examined a Winton and a Packard, finally deciding on the Winton because the company had a ready supply of spare parts that could be delivered to Ashcroft in 24 hours. He purchased two Winton Six seven-passenger cars for $1,500 each.

Williams Lake stockyards, with a Pacific Great Eastern train in the background. The town's population swelled with the coming of the railway, and Williams Lake became the main supply centre for the Cariboo–Chilcotin. *Museum of the Cariboo Chilcotin, Williams Lake photo*

West negotiated the loan of two driver/mechanics to operate the cars for the first season on the Cariboo Road. They arrived in Ashcroft on August 1st and made their first trip up the Cariboo Road on August 5th, thus spelling the end of the colourful days when distinctive red and yellow stagecoaches were the lifeline of the province. There was no shortage of problems with this new mode of transportation, especially on mudding roads, but the BX persisted. Unfortunately, the company lost the mail contract in 1913 and the following year leased its Chilcotin mail delivery out to Tommy Hodgson. This was truly the end of an era. The BX had served the Interior since the gold rush days, and many of the ranches along the Cariboo Road that had served as stopping houses had relied upon the BC Express for income. They had produced food for the passengers and hay for the horses, as well as providing accommodation for passengers and horses alike.

In 1912, Frank Lindsay convinced his father-in-law, Joseph Place, who had a large ranch at Dog Creek, to invest in three Winton Six limousines for use on a stage route between Ashcroft and 150 Mile House. He planned to compete with the BC Express in the passenger and freight business. Unlike the BX, which had horse-drawn stagecoaches to use on difficult roads, Lindsay intended to use his fleet year-round, but his used vehicles proved to be unreliable and next to useless for winter travel. The company was soon in a difficult financial position and Lindsay's wife, Alice, appealed to her father for help. He responded by purchasing the vehicles, bringing them to Dog Creek and selling them for private use. Once again, the BX prevailed. But not for long. In 1920 it lost its mail and freight contracts and quietly went out of business, thus putting an end to over 50 years of service in the BC Interior.

In the more outlying areas, horse-drawn stagecoaches were still necessary as the roads simply did not allow a vehicle to navigate effectively. The stage run from Kamloops to Nicola through Barnhartvale by the Campbell Creek Road to Stump Lake and Quilchena continued to use a horse and wagon until 1918. The halfway point was at Rockford, consisting of a barn, house and cabin on the east side of Stump Lake, where a driver and passengers stayed overnight and a change of horses was made for the remainder of the two-day trip. One winter, driver Albert Anderson was on his way to deliver a letter to the Stump Lake Ranch and decided to take a shortcut across the end of the lake with the stagecoach and horses. The entire rig was too heavy for the ice and broke through. Anderson was obliged to get down and, in freezing water up to his waist, lead the horses out of trouble. Arriving at the ranch house, the soaked, freezing driver was told by the rancher that the delivery price for the letter was far too high and that he wouldn't pay. In what can only be described as a major breach of frontier etiquette, he didn't even ask the driver to come in and warm up. Some days later, Anderson made a second delivery attempt, this time taking the long way around. The rancher reluctantly agreed to pay the original charge but Anderson, none too pleased with his earlier treatment, insisted that the charges were doubled because he had had to take two trips. The mortified rancher forked out the money and hopefully learned his lesson.[10]

Jack Woods was another stagecoach driver, a lifelong bachelor and superb teamster. He had been a teacher on the Prairies before he came to British Columbia in the early 1900s to drive a freight wagon on the Cariboo Road. Eventually he took up a homestead in the Long Lake area south of Kamloops. During the war years, he drove a stagecoach between Kamloops and Nicola to augment his meagre income. He was a crack teamster with up to six very well-cared-for horses. In the summer, when black flies were a nuisance, he covered the horses' noses and ears with pieces of gunny sack to protect against the pests. Jack was quite a character and his confirmed bachelorhood led him to sometimes neglect his personal hygiene. Once, while working in his fields, he caught his leg in the harrows and broke it. Despite the pain, he hobbled to his horse, got on and went to the neighbours who drove him to town. Doc Irving rolled up Jack's pant leg to set the broken limb and commented on the filthy leg that was revealed. "Jack, I'll bet you that's the dirtiest leg in town." Jack quickly retorted, "You lose, Doc," as he rolled up his other pant leg! Another story is told of a neighbour who spent a winter night at Jack's somewhat unkempt cabin. As night fell, Jack began to pull on his heavy coat and chaps, prompting the neighbour to ask him where he was going at that time of night. "I don't know about you," Jack replied, "But I'm going to bed." Apparently, Jack's "pyjamas" were somewhat unconventional.[11]

The Chilcotin was not slow in trying out the new "horseless carriage," despite its rugged roads. When Jack Temple, who owned the Lee place at Hanceville, drove in with a new Cadillac in 1913, he was eager to show off his new toy. He took Herbert Church, who carried the mail from Hanceville to Big Creek once every two weeks, for a ride. They had a most enjoyable ride, but just when Church was prepared to agree that the car was a boon to mankind, the steering jammed and the car went over a low embankment and turned over on the men. Church's left leg was pinned under the frame of the broken windshield, but he managed to free himself and hobble a quarter-mile to Lee's. Men were sent to retrieve Temple—ironically, with a horse and buggy—and extricate him from under the car. Both men had been soaked in gasoline and Church wrote that because he could not strike a light, he had never wanted a smoke so badly in his life.

Even though he walked with a pronounced limp for some time after the accident, Church decided that he should buy a car of his own six years later. He travelled to Vancouver, purchased a seven-passenger Overland and, after a few driving lessons, had the car shipped by rail to Ashcroft. From there, he and his wife proceeded to drive the car to Big Creek. The journey was fraught with adversity and danger. As it was April, the roads were either deep in mud or covered by snow and ice. At one point, the car slid sideways and tipped over on its side. When they got it back on its wheels, they only managed a short distance before it hit a large mudslide. Trying to navigate the slide, they broke the gas line and lost all their fuel. When that was fixed, they still faced the most terrifying part of the journey: the steep, narrow road down to the Fraser River bridge and up the other side toward the Gang Ranch. Church wrote, "We must have been on the very verge of going over the edge several times. At two or three spots where the road had been narrowed by washouts I clearly heard rocks which had been disturbed by the hind wheels rolling down the steep hillside behind me." Church's wife was heard to comment, "It's an awfully long way to the bottom." Church never really recovered from the trip and sold the car a couple of years later.

The first motor car in the Nicola Valley was brought in by W.H. Armstrong, managing director of the Nicola Valley Coal & Coke Company Limited. Not to be outdone, Frank Ward, manager of the Douglas Lake Ranch, bought a 1914 McLaughlin chain-drive touring-model auto. He loved to bring it down to Nicola Lake when the ice was frozen and take the local kids for a drive. He may take the credit of being the first motorist in the province to "do a doughnut" when he found that, by applying the brakes and cranking the steering wheel, he could make the car spin around on the ice. What he didn't realize was that Pete Marquette, the local livery stable owner, had been cutting blocks of ice from the surface of Nicola Lake for Merritt's butcher shops for summer cooling. Frank Ward, with his car full of kids, spun right into the open water with one front wheel of the McLaughlin and came within inches of plunging the entire car into the icy waters. With some embarrassment, Ward had to ask a local rancher to bring his horses, of all things, to pull the car out.[12]

By 1917, Hugh Bayliffe of the Chilanko Ranch had a Dodge touring car and soon cars were appearing everywhere in the Interior. There were Studebakers, Chevrolets, Model T Fords and various other makes. Gasoline was cheap, so large cars were popular. The Model T was popular but the gravity-fed gas lines were a real problem. If the fuel was low, the cars did not have enough gas to climb the steep hills. The only solution was to turn the car around and back up the hill. But the worst problem was the rocky roads that caused frequent flat tires. Inner tubes were patched until they began to look like patchwork quilts. Cars were generally put away for the winter because the deep snow made driving impossible. They were winterized by having all the tires removed before being put up on blocks; the battery would be stored inside until spring. Of course, spring, with its mudholes, presented new challenges. Undeterred, intrepid drivers would forge on, equipped with block and tackle to pull them out of mudholes and, more often than not, the only way to get out of a hole was to enlist the help of a nearby rancher with—you guessed it—a team of versatile, and never slowed down by mud, workhorses.

Keeping in Touch

Another indication that "civilization" was beginning to reach the more isolated areas of the province was when BC Telephone began to string telephone lines on Jack pines from Clinton to the Gang Ranch and then on via Dog Creek and Alkali Lake to Williams Lake. The system consisted of a single wire with a buzzer that would signal when it was in use so that telegrams could be transmitted when it was not being used for conversation. A horn-like gadget called a "howler" was used to signal its status but it could also double as a loudspeaker since every sound coming along the line was audible. This distinct lack of privacy ensured that the more conventional systems of communicating secrets—that is, word of mouth and mail—were not immediately threatened.

A story is told of one of the "school marms" in the Cariboo being helped onto her saddle horse in the twilight by two of the local boys. She found the saddle particularly uncomfortable and, upon arriving home, realized the problem. The boys had put the saddle on backwards and the teacher had ridden home with the cantle in the front and the horn in the back. When she discovered this, she got on the phone to complain to their mother. But the howlers of every telephone in the district broadcast her anger and the word spread like wildfire so the entire countryside soon knew (and approved) of the prank.

When the telephone reached the Chilcotin, the modern contraption was the source of some concern over privacy issues. One young prankster was fond of calling up women early in the morning and saying, "Good morning, my dear, how pretty you look this morning!" His reply was usually silence from the other end as the woman in question considered his statement and then haltingly responded, "You can't see me, can you?"

As interest in the new technology spread, Quesnel telegraph operator Hope Patenaude decided to order one of these new contraptions. The telephone was duly boxed up and shipped from the coast but never arrived. Patenaude contacted the shippers and asked for a description of the box the telephone had been shipped in. The mystery was solved when he was told it had been packed carefully in a government whisky box. Some hopeful thief had seen the box and thought he was onto a good thing, only to find the "whisky" was not very consumable. No doubt he had pitched the entire package into a ditch.

The Native people of the Interior were slow in taking advantage of the new technology, showing some reluctance to deal with the new talking machine, and making a call from one reserve to another was not always a simple matter. First of all, a call would have to be made to the subscriber nearest to the reserve required, asking that a messenger be sent to the wanted party to request they come to the telephone. This might take up to a couple of days to happen. Then a time had to be arranged for both parties to be available to make the connection. Only after days of arrangements could the two parties have their conversation, most often of less than five minutes' duration. Not surprisingly, most Native people preferred the time-honoured method of sending messages via travellers on horseback and used the telephone only when they were not in a hurry to communicate.

British Ranchers

From the beginning of ranching in British Columbia, British immigrants brought with them some of the practices and techniques of caring for cattle that had been practised in Britain for hundreds of years. Many of these were adopted by the early drovers and cattlemen, making British Columbia ranching techniques different in some ways from the practices of the rest of North America. Stock dogs, which had been used for centuries to herd cattle and sheep in Britain, were readily accepted and it soon became obvious that a good dog could take the place of several men in herding cattle. The British practice of moving cattle seasonally also caught on in British Columbia. Cattle would be moved up to the high country for summer grazing and rounded up and brought down to the lowlands for winter feeding. These and other practices gave British Columbia ranching a unique blend of the old and the new worlds.

The practice of British families sending their younger sons to the ranches of British Columbia to learn ranching had begun in the 1880s but persisted well into the 20th century. Many of these "mud pups," as they were called by the locals, worked for nothing until they learned the business and went on to become excellent ranchers. Unlike the "remittance men" who regularly received money from home and had no incentive to work at anything, most mud pups worked hard and were soon happily accepted into the ranching community.[13]

Everywhere they lived, the British brought with them the customs and attitudes of home. Hugh and Gertrude Bayliffe, who had lived in the Alexis Creek area of the Chilcotin since the 1880s, still dressed for dinner at a table set with the finest silver and china. Doris Butler, whose husband, William "Bertie," had come from Wiltshire to the Westwold area, recalled that, despite the hardships of ranch life, "I always changed in the afternoon and never

on any account went without afternoon tea." The Bayliffes encouraged polo playing, which caught on locally—perhaps not surprising considering its need for highly skilled horsemen.

Many of the names of locations and towns in the ranching country were British in origin, named after individuals or places. This trend continued as more and more British arrived in the area and even long-established place names were altered by the newcomers. A good example was when Harry and Louise Coldwell, from Jesmond near Newcastle upon Tyne, England, purchased a south Cariboo roadhouse that had been called the Mountain House since the earliest gold rush days. The roadhouse was the overnight stopping place for the Dog Creek Stage, driven by Joe Place. The Coldwells' hospitality was well known and meals were a sociable affair with every guest seated around a huge kitchen table with Harry at one end carving the meat and Louise at the other dishing out the vegetables. When a post office was established at the roadhouse in 1919, the Coldwells insisted on calling the office "Jesmond" and, reluctantly, the locals agreed. The original Mountain House building burned down in 1921 but the name Jesmond stuck and the post office kept the name until it closed in 1960.

Captain Geoffrey Launcelot Watson

Captain Geoffrey Launcelot Watson was a six-foot-six former British army officer and an accomplished horseman and crack shot. He was educated at Eton and enlisted to fight in the Boer War at the

Kathleen Newton riding sidesaddle. Kathleen was born in England and married Reginald Fitz-Nigel Newton, who ranched at the mouth of the Chilco River.
Museum of the Cariboo Chilcotin, Williams Lake photo

age of 20. After the war, he travelled to Canada and, while touring British Columbia, fell in love with the Cariboo. It was rumoured that he came from the Watson Scotch Whisky family and there is no doubt that he came from a very wealthy background. He was able to acquire 50,000 acres of rolling Cariboo ranchland just north of 100 Mile House, some through a military grant but most through outright purchase. Watson stocked his ranch with a herd of 10,000 Highland cattle and constructed a huge log barn, a slaughterhouse, bunkhouses, an icehouse and a store on the property. But his most impressive addition was a beautiful three-storey house, designed by a Victoria architect and furnished with the finest goods money could buy, all freighted in from the railhead at Ashcroft. Watson intended to bring his bride-to-be from England to this lovely home and live as the lord and lady of the manor. But his fiancée was not in the least interested in emigrating to "the colonies" and the wedding was called off.

Watson called his property the Highland Ranch to reflect his Scottish ancestry and in recognition of the purebred Highland cattle that stocked the ranch. He was also an admirer of fine horseflesh and imported 100 purebred Clydesdale horses from Scotland. But Watson was far from a snob. He mixed easily in the community and was known for taking the local children for rides in his sleigh pulled by imported reindeer. He was greatly loved by the local Native community for providing them with food in times of difficulty and employing the men to work on his ranch. These cowboys were all excellent horsemen and could be seen on Watson's regular cattle drives to the railhead in Ashcroft. When war broke out in 1914, he was quick to return to England to enlist. Unfortunately he was killed in action in 1917 and his empire was sold off in parcels. His Highland cattle were soon replaced with the more popular Herefords and Shorthorns and, in 1983, his beautiful house, by then fully restored, burned to the ground.[14]

Gordon Farwell and Gerald Blenkinsop

Another British rancher, Gordon Farwell, from a well-to-do family in Leicestershire, arrived in the Chilcotin in 1903. His father had paid Fred Beaumont, who owned the Beaver Ranch, to accept him as a mud pup. Farwell took to ranching like a duck to water and, being of a cheerful disposition, didn't take long to fit in with the rough and ready cowboys at the Beaver Ranch. Initially he was green as grass but it wasn't long before he was able to ride and rope with the best of them. In fact, his horsemanship was officially acknowledged as the best in 1913, when he won the Chilcotin Ranchers Cup at the annual race meet on Becher's Prairie on a horse named Fox. Farwell purchased his own place on a flat beside the Chilcotin River that is known to this day as Farwell Canyon. The location was sheltered in the winter but could be incredibly hot in the summer as there was no wind and the heat would reflect off the canyon walls. Farwell decided to call his place The Pothole and began to develop the land, planting alfalfa on the fertile bottomland that he irrigated with water dammed in the creek above.

In 1912, Farwell met and formed a partnership with Gerald Blenkinsop, another Englishman from Warwickshire. He too was a mud pup, having come to work on the Chilco Ranch for Claude Wilson in 1907. Blenkinsop had ridden to the hounds with Wilson in England, so was an accomplished rider. The transition to a western saddle and learning to rope cattle was an easy one for him. After five years of "training" at the Chilco Ranch, Blenkinsop joined Farwell at the Pothole and they remained friends for the rest of their lives.

The partners built separate homes on the ranch and raised horses. Blenkinsop also drove a freight wagon on the Cariboo Road for extra income. In 1914, he married Madeline Wheeler, nicknamed "Queenie." She had come from England to work for Mrs. Cotton, who was married to yet another mud pup, Robert Cecil Cotton of the Cotton Ranch. Queenie was a talented pianist and, as a wedding present, Lois Vedan, who had owned the Pothole before Farwell, purchased a Heintzman grand piano for her. Transporting the huge piano in a wagon down the steep narrow road into the Pothole and across the old bridge was a hair-raising adventure but, from then on, beautiful music enhanced the lives of all those who lived and worked on the ranch. Not to be outdone, the next year Gordon Farwell married an Irish woman, Annie Christie Riley, and the couples lived happily in their homes in what they came to call Happy Valley. The two families sold the Pothole to the Gang Ranch in 1919 and moved to Sugar Cane Jack's, a higher and cooler location in the Big Creek area. Six years later, the Farwells sold their share to the Blenkinsops and moved to Victoria. But the Blenkinsops stayed on the Chilcotin for the rest of their lives.

Colonel Cecil Whitaker

G. Cecil Whitaker, a well-to-do Englishman whose family owned large estates in Hampshire, was captivated by the beautiful open valley at Grande Prairie (now Westwold). In 1911, he began acquiring land in the valley, purchasing first the property originally ranched by Herbert Guernsey and later the Adelphi Ranch, originally owned by Walter Homfray. The Adelphi Ranch also included the Adelphi Hotel as well as a racetrack, complete with a judges' stand and grandstand. Whitaker changed the name of the property to Pylewell, after the Whitaker family home, Pylewell Estate, and laid out a townsite, complete with street names. His intention was to bring in British settlers and set up his own estate in Canada. Despite the fact that the Adelphi Hotel was less than 20 years old, he constructed a second hotel on the property, the Pylewell. At that time, the Canadian National Railway was planning to construct a branch line from Kamloops to Armstrong. Whitaker had offered a free right-of-way for the railway and was assured that the new rail line would run right through his property. He established a weaving business to provide winter work for his tenants and brought in equipment that he placed in a weaving house on part of his ranch. To operate the weaving business he brought in two Scottish families, the Donald McLeans and the Donald McKenzies from the Isle of Lewis and constructed houses for the two families nearby. In an effort to promote the business, Whitaker had Donald McLean demonstrate weaving at the Vancouver Exhibition in 1913. Although it led to a few sales, the business never caught on as Whitaker had hoped. By 1915, the McKenzies had left and Donald McLean was feeding pigs on the ranch. A few of the lots at Pylewell sold but the coming of the First World War and the general slowing of immigration stalled the demand for property. The war also meant that plans for the construction of the railway through Grande Prairie were halted indefinitely. At the outbreak of the war, Whitaker returned to England and served with the Coldstream Guards. He saw considerable action at the front and was promoted to captain in 1916 and major in 1919. When he returned in 1919, Whitaker tried unsuccessfully to sell the Adelphi Hotel. Although work had started on the railway, progress was extremely slow in the postwar economy and the line was not completed until 1925. In the meantime, Whitaker was slowly selling off his holdings. In 1927 he sold off all his cattle when the winter pasture he was leasing was rented out to the Clemitsons, leaving him with no place to winter his cattle. Whitaker's dream of a British enclave in the heart of British Columbia was fading. Despite numerous challenges, Whitaker's on-site manager, Frank Gordon, did his best to keep the ranch viable. The Pylewell Hotel burned down in 1943 but the Adelphi Hotel is still standing. The last of Colonel Whitaker's holdings in the Westwold valley were sold off in the 1940s.

Eric Collier

Born in Northampton, England, in 1903, Eric Collier came to make his life in the rugged Cariboo–Chilcotin in 1920. Harry Marriott, who had come from England many years earlier, described his first impressions of Collier:

One evening as I was splitting some firewood outside the log cabin, getting ready to make my supper, I heard a noise and saw a young man coming towards me. He had riding britches and leggings on him, which at once told me he must be an Englishman or a land surveyor. He was a wiry built young fellow, and of course I knew he was a stranger. Looking up at me with a half-smile on his face he said, "Are you by any chance called Harry Marriott?" I said, "Yes, that's me, and all that's left of him." He told me he was my cousin, Eric Collier, from Northamptonshire in faraway England, and that he had come out to British Columbia with a view of learning the cow business.[15]

Marriott confessed that he had no money to pay him but agreed to teach Collier about ranching and provide room and board in return for free labour. Over the next few weeks, the two men put up 40 tons of hay. Collier stayed on for the summer and then went to Riske Creek to work in the store owned by Fred Becher. He built up his savings for a few years and began looking for land of his own. In 1929, newly married to Lillian Ross, he moved to an isolated area at Madden Lake. Two years later, in spite of his wife's hip deformity due to a childhood accident, the couple took a wagon, three horses and their 18-month-old son, Veasy, along with a tent, some provisions and $33, and reached the Stack Valley where they lived in an abandoned cabin built by a trapper and carpenter called Tom Evans. In a few years, they relocated to Meldrum Creek, 10 miles away, where they lived in a tent while they built their own cabin. Collier and his wife had promised her 97-year-old Native grandmother, LaLa, to bring the beavers back to the area that she knew as a child before the white man came. Collier imported several pairs of beavers, and raised the area's water table sufficiently to reinstate the beaver population. Eventually beavers were so numerous that they became his most important fur pelt on his trapline.

In 1939 Collier sold his favourite saddle horse so that he could purchase a radio and hear news of the war that was breaking out in Europe. In 1946, he became the first president of the B.C. Trappers Association, an organization he co-founded with Ed Bobbs. With the second guiding licence to be issued in the Chilcotin, Collier earned a meagre income to supplement his trapping and hunting. He perfected the Conibear trap, a more humane trap that is still used today. Collier was an excellent writer and regularly published short stories in *Outdoor Life* magazine, but his bestselling book, *Three Against the Wilderness,* was his most powerful statement on the theme of conservation. His strong opinions on conservation occasionally caused him to confront the government's Game Branch, but his point of view was always respected and his quiet strength gave him a reputation as a true gentleman. The Colliers retired to the Riske Creek area in 1964 and built a small house to live in. Eric was quite proud of the knotty pine board wall that he added to the house until a local who was visiting remarked, "It's too bad about all the knots in that wood. Are you going to paper over it?" Collier, ever the gentleman, just smiled. He died at Riske Creek on March 15, 1966. The *Williams Lake Tribune*'s obituary stated, "To watch Eric Collier stride through the woods was a joy to behold . . . Gun crooked comfortably in his arm he moved along as easily as the city dweller would stroll down Granville Street." [16]

Returning Soldiers

When more than four years of war came to a close on November 11, 1918, the thousands of young men from the British Columbia Interior who had fought in the mud of France and Belgium began to trickle home. By the time the war had reached its end, British Columbia had contributed 55,570 men, over 12 percent of its entire population and the highest per capita enlistment in Canada, to the war effort. A staggering 6,225 had lost their lives and another 13,607 had been wounded, a casualty rate of almost 36 percent! But the province could point with pride to 14 Victoria Crosses and countless other honours that its citizens had won. British Columbia had done its part and the ranching areas of the province had contributed disproportionately to the cause.

Many of the men who returned home were never the same again, having been mutilated in body or in mind. Some returned minus a limb or an eye, or severely disfigured, but often the damage was not immediately obvious. Thousands had their lungs damaged by mustard gas and even more suffered psychological damage that they carried with them for the rest of their lives. The concept of "post-traumatic stress" was unheard of and the army did not know how to deal with those soldiers who suffered from "shell shock" caused by the horrors of trench warfare. Equally confusing for the returning soldiers were the changes in Canadian life that had taken place since they had left. Everything from the length of skirts to the value of money had been transformed by the war years. The "temporary" measure of income tax, which had been established to help the war effort, remained in place. Harry Marriott was one of the lucky ones who returned relatively unscathed, but even he had to make major adjustments upon his return home.

> I was hit by shrapnel a couple of times, but not seriously, and I was scared to death a million times, but that was a daily diet for most all of the boys in

action . . . I had one hell of a time getting settled down again, for a matter of a month or two, after getting back to Crow's Bar. It was a big change from the rush, roar of action of army life—the excitement and high pitch of armies in action, and the "eat, drink and be merry, because tomorrow you may die" atmosphere for quite a long spell. All these were a considerable change to a set-up of being alone most of the time, and being my own boss, with decisions to make once more.[17]

The Canadian government set up the Department of Soldiers' Civil Re-establishment in 1918 to handle the major problem of returning Canadian servicemen to civilian life following the war. One of its branches was the Soldier Settlement Board, established to assist returned servicemen to set up farms and ranches. The Board would give assistance to any man who had served abroad with the Canadian Expeditionary Force, to any former Canadian serviceman who had not left Canada but was receiving a service pension, to any member of the Allied forces who had lived inside Canada before the war, or to any member of the Imperial or Dominion forces who had served his country and had since immigrated to Canada. Those who fell into the last category were required to work on a farm or ranch for a while to prove that they could do the work and that they had enough capital to establish themselves. They were also required to make a down payment of 20 percent for land, stock, implements and buildings.

As the above suggests, the Board was concerned about turning young men loose on their own land without first making sure that they were not destined for failure. Applicants for a loan to purchase land were also investigated for their fitness, character, assets and abilities. Quite often, if it didn't look like they had enough farming experience, they were asked to work on a farm or ranch and were paid allowances to help them through this period, especially if they had families.

By 1921, about 43,000 loans had been given out. Loans of up to $7,500 were made for the purchase of land, including up to $4,500 for land, $2,000 for stock and $1,000 for improvements. If a soldier already owned land, he could receive a loan of up to $5,000 for livestock, equipment and improvements and to pay off existing debt.

The Prairie provinces were the most popular provinces for resettlement, followed by British Columbia. All settlers helped by the Soldier Settlement Board were visited regularly by field supervisors to check on their progress and to give advice. Unfortunately, most of the good ranchland in British Columbia was already taken, but the Board purchased what good ranchland was available. In the Grande Prairie area, where the Board purchased several parcels of land, brothers Harold and Syd Culling obtained land and Ernest Noble added an additional 160 acres to his small ranch.

Once the soldiers returned, they faced another life-threatening situation—the Spanish flu. In the spring of 1918, many soldiers in the trenches in France had become ill, complaining of a sore throat, headaches and a loss of appetite. Although the illness appeared to be highly infectious, recovery was rapid and doctors gave it the name of three-day fever. At first doctors could not identify the illness but eventually they decided it was a new strain of influenza. The soldiers named it Spanish Flu but there is no evidence that it really did originate from that country. In fact, in Spain they called it French Flu.

For the next few months soldiers continued to be infected with the virus but there were very few fatalities. However, in the summer of 1918 the symptoms became much more severe. About one-fifth of the victims developed pneumonia or blood-poisoning. A large percentage of these men died. This second wave of the epidemic spread quickly. In one sector of the Western Front over 70,000 US troops were hospitalized and nearly one-third of them failed to recover. By the end of the summer the virus had reached the German army. The virus created serious problems for the German military leadership as they found it impossible to replace their sick and dying soldiers. The infection had already reached Germany and over 400,000 civilians died of the disease in 1918. The influenza epidemic travelled with the soldiers to Britain and soon spread to other towns and cities. During the next few months the virus killed 228,000 people in Britain. This was the highest mortality rate for any epidemic since the outbreak of cholera in 1849.

The epidemic soon spread with the returning soldiers to most of the countries of the world. British Columbia was not spared. The flu quickly reached the Interior and, despite the relative isolation, the ranching community was soon hit. Grande Prairie was severely hit. In a five-week period in late 1918, six people died from the flu in the small community. With all the young men either away to war, sick with the disease or staying isolated, there was no one available for grave digging, so family members had to dig the graves of their loved ones.

Some stories of self-sacrifice and heroism in dealing with the disease rivalled the most heroic deeds of the war. On the remote Gang Ranch, the Native people, whose living conditions were particularly miserable, were hit hard. When word reached the ranch headquarters that the well-known and respected Kalese family was suffering, Mrs. Anderson, who had some experience in dealing with the sick, could not sit by idly and watch. She gathered some extra clothing in a sack and headed to the Kalese family home by sleigh, a full day's travel over the snow. When she reached the one-room cabin, she found two people dead already and five children and three adults sick with the flu. With a Native boy as a helper, she dragged the two dead bodies out onto the porch where the -20°F weather kept the bodies well preserved. Then she set about caring for the living. After cleaning the cabin, she found some deer meat and made a soup that she spoon-fed to her patients. Day after day, she persevered and, when a cowboy from the Gang Ranch arrived two weeks later, he found that Mrs. Anderson had not lost one of her patients.

It has been estimated that over 70 million people died of the influenza pandemic throughout the world. In India alone, more people died of influenza than were killed worldwide during the entire First World War.

Organizations

Ranchers tend to be an independent lot. The essence of their business means that, for all intents and purposes, they are pretty much on their own against nature and the forces of the outside world. Although they attach great value to neighbours, they would rather not see the government too involved in their lives. This independence tends to carry over into the area of organizations and associations.

Following a call by C.W. Hadwen at the 1897 BC Fruit Growers' annual meeting, the provincial government agreed to set up a system of local Farmers' Institutes in any locality where 15 farmers petitioned for one. Despite a slow start, by 1914 there were over 80 Farmers' Institutes throughout the province. These organizations were designed primarily to educate farmers in the latest techniques of farming and animal husbandry. As well, the Farmers' Institutes sought to promote community growth in the building of schools, formation of literary clubs and other social activities.

The Farmers' Institute played an important role in most communities. Cattlemen could buy purebred cattle, seed and stumping powder through the institute. Stumping powder was used for removing larger stumps from the hayfields. A space was dug between two large roots and packed with the powder, a fuse and a blasting cap. The resulting concussion would blow a stump almost out of the ground so that a team could pull it the rest of the way out.

Members of the Farmers' Institutes would meet regularly to exchange information and ideas on various topics. They would arrange fall fairs so that farmers and ranchers could show their animals and produce before experienced judges. Farmers' Institutes would also organize to maintain the telephone network, arranging for each farmer or rancher to maintain a section of phone line and to patrol the line—which was most often strung on trees in the early days—looking for breaks.

The Rose Hill Farmers' Institute is typical. It was founded in 1911 and is still around today. Over the years, it has carried on its mandate of promoting the community and improving farming. Some of its activities included petitioning the provincial government for a well-drilling machine for use in the community, purchasing bailer twine in bulk from suppliers for reduced prices, organizing a seed fair, initiating grasshopper control in the district and putting on numerous fundraisers for families in need.

But there was an even more pressing need for ranchers to get together for marketing purposes. Ranchers realized that they could not fight their battles alone against the government, railway companies, meat packers and consumers. It was not difficult to see that cattle growers were being taken advantage of by buyers and that it was time for them to get together to present a united front against the powers that were determined to keep beef prices low and profits high for the corporate giants such as Burns and Swifts Meats.

As early as 1889, the BC Cattle Association was formed in Kamloops when a bunch of Thompson and Okanagan area ranchers got together to try and organize. But, like so many cattle organizations that were to follow, the membership did not grow large enough to have any influence or to make a difference. In 1914, Cariboo ranchers formed the Cariboo Cattlemen's Association, and that same year the Interior Stock Raisers Association of BC was formed to bring a united voice from the ranchers. This organization joined with the parallel BC Stock Breeders Association, which was more interested in improving beef breeds, in 1919. This Kamloops-based organization, in conjunction with the provincial department of agriculture, organized the very successful Kamloops Bull Sale in 1919. The bull sale was held in early spring when ranchers were looking for new bulls for their herds. The event also included judging of purebred Hereford, Shorthorn, Angus and Red Poll stock and then auctioning them off. The sale has remained an institution in British Columbia ranching since that day and is still one of the great social events of the year for many ranchers.

The earliest bull sales were somewhat "catch as catch can" affairs as ranchers had little time to examine their prospective purchases. One rancher complained to the Douglas Lake Ranch that one of their bulls that he had purchased had only one testicle. Frank Ward, the manager of the Douglas Lake Ranch, wrote in reply:

These bulls had a very hard deal before going to the sale, and were picked out in very cold weather, and driven over to Kamloops, a distance of 75 miles through deep snow, and as the cold has, as a rule, a decided effect on the testicle of a bull, it is not so much to be wondered at as you think, that such a thing might be overlooked. If the bull is wrong, we will appoint somebody to examine him, and will replace the bull by exchange next spring or refund your money and turn the one you have over to the butcher. We regret very much that such a thing should have occurred.[18]

The rancher, somewhat taken aback by this generous offer, admitted that he was a victim of his own carelessness and decided to keep the bull as he seemed to be performing well enough with what he had.

Chapter Two

BOOM YEARS

It was the beginning of February in the high country and the three cowboys were alone in their cabin high up on the Interior Plateau. They had been feeding 200 head of cattle from the large haystack in the nearby field since the middle of December. The winter had been tolerable and the hay was holding out well, but February began with bone-chilling temperatures of minus -60°F. Each morning the cowboys would bundle up in all their available winter clothing. Cowboy hats had long been abandoned for thick woollen caps with ear flaps. Even then, the trip to the haystack on the hay rack was tortuous. Two of the cowboys would wrestle with each other to keep warm, but the third clutched the reins of the hay rack with wooden hands and faced forward. By the time they reached the stack, his face would be white and frozen. In those days, the prevailing wisdom was that to alleviate the freezing it was necessary to rub snow on the exposed skin. So the two somewhat warm cowboys would rub snow on their partner's face to keep it from freezing. Soon all three cowboys would be pitching hay from the stack and warming up with the exertion. Then they would head out of the hay yard and feed the hungry cattle, who never would have survived for any length of time in that weather without the precious hay. The cowboys would chop holes in the ice of the water hole and then travel back to their cabin to try and keep warm until the next day's feeding. If they paused to think about it, they would take some comfort in the thought that, all through the cattle country, cowboys like themselves were suffering through the same ordeal. But it would all be worthwhile when the cattle came out of winter with fat on their bones, ready for the spring grasses.

Haystack near Okanagan Lake. Note the "hay sloop" in the foreground. *Historic O'Keefe Ranch photo*

The 1920s were a time of significant change for the ranchers of the British Columbia Interior. To begin with, the world had changed with the First World War. In a way, it had lost its innocence. Thousands of young men returned from the war jaded and disillusioned with life, and this attitude spread into the society of the day. Life in the trenches had been one of "eat, drink and be merry, because tomorrow you may die." This "live for today" approach to life was brought back by the returning soldiers, colouring much of what was to be justifiably called the Roaring Twenties. While this attitude was much more prominent in the larger urban settings, it could still be seen, in a more subtle way, in the ranching community.

Ranch Consolidation

With the opening of the Pacific Great Eastern Railway in 1917 and the advent of motorized transport, the ranches along the Cariboo Road soon found themselves without a ready market for the hay and garden produce that they once supplied to travellers. This loss of extra income resulted in a basic change in the traditional ranching model that had prevailed since the early gold rush days. Ranchers were forced to depend entirely upon cattle for their income. The re-orientation to cattle ranching exclusively was not entirely successful. Smaller ranches simply did not have enough land or cattle to generate the income they needed to survive. This resulted in a

Chilco Ranch, early 1920s. The ranch eventually encompassed 23,000 acres, with grazing rights on another 827,000 acres. *Museum of the Cariboo Chilcotin, Williams Lake photo*

move from small ranch units to larger holdings. Although the consolidation of holdings had been going on for several decades, and most of the large ranches had taken shape before the war, there was an increased trend toward the establishment of medium- and large-sized ranches after the war. More and more small ranchsteads were abandoned as available rangeland was consolidated under a single "home ranch" that served as the headquarters for a large number of once independent holdings.

Many homesteaders found themselves unable to make a go of things on their small holdings and put their places up for sale. In such cases larger adjoining or neighbourhood ranches often purchased them, even if it meant borrowing the money. One of the large ranches in the area south of Kamloops was the Willow Ranch, owned by Joe Bulman. During the war years, he bought up numerous smaller ranches until he held about 40,000 acres in two different locations. One of the settlers that he bought out was a man named Higgins, who had a quarter section of land and a few head of cattle. The purchase was paid for in cash and, when Higgins went to Kamloops to sign the papers, word of the sale got out to the gamblers of the town. The deal completed and the money in his pocket, Higgins was walking down the street in Kamloops when he was greeted by a "friend" who just happened to be one of the local poker sharks. He invited the cash-rich former homesteader to join him in a friendly game of poker. The boys around the table knew how fat Higgins' wallet was and figured they had better play this fish very carefully and slowly. So they let him win a few hands to encourage his participation. After he had won a couple hundred dollars, Higgins looked at his watch and

jumped up out of his chair. "Sorry, boys," he proclaimed, "I've got to run to catch the train for the coast. Thanks for the game." As Higgins gathered his cash and headed out the door, the poker sharks were outraged. They were even more outraged when they learned that Higgins had been a sailor for many years and was a poker player of some repute.[1]

Another typical mega-ranch was the Chilco Ranch, across the river from Hanceville, which came to comprise five formerly independent ranches. The ranch started in 1884 when Mike Minton, a big, friendly Irishman pre-empted on the bench land on the south side of the Chilcotin River. At that time, there was no bridge, so the river had to be forded when it was low or crossed by canoe when the water was high. Twelve years later, Minton sold out to Claude Wilson, an Englishman who gave the ranch its name. Wilson bought out several neighbours and, in partnership with the Tsilhqot'in Natives from the Stone Reserve, set up a 20-mile-long irrigation system, consisting of ditches and flumes, from Big Creek. The system delivered water to the Stone Reserve, the main Chilco hayfields and another hayfield owned by the ranch. In 1909, the ranch was purchased by Joe Trethewey, who had made his money in logging in Ontario. Trethewey bought up all the adjacent land he could get his hands on, eventually owning 23,000 acres, and built 90 miles of fences. He owned over 600 head of Hereford and Galloway cattle and 400 head of horses. Eventually the Chilco Ranch had grazing rights on 850,000 acres.

Trethewey hadn't quite got logging out of his blood and so he set up a sawmill on the ranch. But it was not without its problems and was known to drive the owner to fits of anger. On one particularly disastrous day when everything seemed to be going wrong, Trethewey lost it entirely and fired the entire crew. He shouted at one of the surprised crewmen, "Take your partner and get out of here!" The man meekly replied, "But I don't have a partner." Trethewey shouted back, "Well, I'll damned soon find you one."

Another mega-ranch was the Felker Ranch at Lac la Hache, which eventually comprised nine separate holdings. However, these ranches, including the Gang Ranch—which controlled close to a million acres through deeded land and grazing leases—and the Chilco Ranch, were not the norm.

Rodeo

When the various ranches in a district came together for roundup and branding, the skill of an individual cowboy was highlighted in front of his peers. The work of rounding up cattle, separating the livestock of one ranch from the others, roping and branding the calves, or cutting out marketable animals for shipment required strength, agility and split-second judgement. Naturally each outfit was anxious to make a good showing of its cowboys' skill in handling cattle. "Dude" Lavington wrote about the friendly competition that lurked under the surface when he was branding with the legendary Floyd "Pan" Phillips who had been born in Illinois and came to the Blackwater River area in the 1930s. Lavington was working for the Frontier Cattle Company, owned by Phillips and his partner, Rich Hobson. "I had heard a great deal about these American cowboys and their roping and I was afraid to let the Canadians down. I had been a pretty fair roper but for quite a few years we had so little stock to practice on—mainly roping a horse that was hard to catch, or practice roping on a pack in a string of pack horses—so I was pretty rusty. But now I had not only the opportunity but the necessity to rope fairly well."[2]

Lavington finally got the opportunity to show his ability and made the best of it. "Pan was mostly head roping with damn few misses and keeping two crews working, all we could stand with those big hefty calves. Once in a while I noticed Pan do what he called a 'California Twist.' Neat throw for corral work. I practiced it myself afterwards . . . We helped get the beef herd separated and started out with the chuck wagon and all the cowboys first, then went to branding. This time I did the roping. But I was a heel roper and by now pretty handy. I roped thirty-four without a miss. Aikens kept a tally on my performance. So I guess I didn't let the Canadian cowboys down too badly."[3]

Around the campfire at night, talk always got around to who was the best bronc buster or roper in the district. Roping prowess was something that could be demonstrated in a working situation and, as the above account shows, someone would be designated to keep a tally. Roping the calves by the back legs, or "heeling," was considered easier on the calf as it allowed the cowboy to drag the calf backwards to the branding fire instead of choking it with a rope around the neck. Bronc riding was a different matter. Most really difficult horses were kept away from a working situation like roundup. So, when branding was finished for the day, particularly "rank" horses would be found and the best cowboys in each outfit picked to compete. Inevitably money would be placed on the outcome. Generally horses would be snubbed to a post or thrown down so that they could be saddled and then the cowboy would jump aboard and ride them until they stopped bucking or until he was thrown. There was no such thing as a timed event. Horses would be ridden to a standstill, whether it took a minute or an hour. There was no prize money for the winning cowboy, only for the gamblers, but "bragging rights" counted for a lot and the winner would be bought drinks by his backers the next time the boys were in town.

Rodeo in the Merritt area in the early 1930s. Before rodeo arenas were used, spectators would circle their wagons and cars to form an enclosure. *Historic O'Keefe Ranch photo*

"Jackpot rodeos," where cowboys from all over would come to a central location on a Sunday or during downtime at the ranch and each would throw in a set amount of money, with the winner taking the pot, soon sprang up. These were community events and people from all the nearby ranches would come to visit and watch the excitement. Sandy Brent, who was raised at his grandfather's Shingle Creek Ranch in the South Okanagan, talked about these jackpot rodeos.

> The Natives used to come on Sundays and we'd have riding, chutes and things. Lots of riding! There was no pick-up men, you just got off yourself, or stayed on. They always had pick-up men in the rodeos, but here they figured to make a good rider out of you, you had to get off yourself. Some Sundays, Grandpa and I used to feed fifty people all from Summerland . . . Jimmy Fife would bring up a whole track of four-horse teams with wagons and with people on it. On Saturday night they'd have a little dance in the house. One time they had as many as a hundred people there. Dick Gilridge . . . was a violinist. He'd play the gramophone and he'd fiddle along with the gramophone. The horses we used as bucking stock were cayuses from off the range . . . We'd go through about fifteen or twenty horses. We bucked them out twice, or whatever they needed. The good ones we'd buck about five or six times.[4]

These jackpot rodeos began to evolve into full blown rodeos. In the earliest years, people would park their wagons or automobiles in a circle in the middle of a field and that would become the rodeo grounds. Eventually these gatherings became annual events. The Williams Lake Stampede lists its first "official" rodeo as taking place in 1920 but most old-timers agreed that it really started a year earlier when ranches from the area gathered for a weekend of bronc and steer riding, roping and horse races. At that time, Williams Lake was little more than a collection of a few ramshackle buildings clustered around the Borland Ranch house. The property had just been purchased by the Pacific Great Eastern Railway, which was slowly being constructed through the Cariboo at the time. Hundreds of people from all over the Cariboo and Chilcotin gathered on the flats beside the north end of Williams Lake and a small town of tents and wagons sprung up overnight. There were no fences or grandstands, just a few corrals where livestock could be kept until needed. After a day of competition in which Native and white cowboys showed their talents, an all-night dance was held in the Borland House. The following day saw a vast exodus of families, tired and bleary-eyed but determined that they were going to do this again next year. And so the institution of the Williams Lake Stampede, sometimes called the Cariboo Stampede, was born.

By 1920, the town of Williams Lake had grown to contain hotels, banks and stores surrounded by houses. The Stampede was organized along the

Horse race at the Penticton rodeo grounds, 1918. Horse races were a standard feature of early rodeos. *Okanagan Archives Trust photo*

Tent City at the Williams Lake Stampede in the early 1920s. Hundreds of people from all over the Cariboo and Chilcotin gathered for rodeo excitement and socializing. *Museum of the Cariboo Chilcotin, Williams Lake photo*

lines of the previous year's and, with the help of the town's growing merchant population, prize money for the winning cowboys was topped up to make the purses even more attractive. From the outset, the Stampede was a little different from other rodeos. One event, the Roman Race, had the riders standing with their feet on the backs of two horses as they galloped and jostled down the track. The Mountain Race was even more terrifying. It featured a hair-raising plunge at full gallop down Fox Mountain to the Stampede grounds. The event was first run in 1922 and was the climax of the Stampede until 1953. Stampede organizer Jo Flieger laid out the course, which included a drop down a narrow, steep gulch that could only be entered via a narrow ridge where there was room for about eight riders abreast. Once down the gulch, the riders had to head through brush, fallen trees and loose gravel to another ridge and down another steep slope before crossing the Cariboo highway. The final dash to the finish at the Stampede grounds had all the spectators wild with excitement.

One of the few women to attempt the race was Ollie Matheson (née Curtis), who had been brought up at the Alkali Lake Ranch. She first competed in the race when she was 17 years old in the 1920s, coming second or third each time. She described the thrill involved. "I liked it. It was a challenge. But my dad almost had a fit . . . and so did some of the cowboys . . . You had to have a heavy, well-built, very sure-footed horse. There was no trail, just markers to guide the riders so they wouldn't get hung up in the bush."[5]

Needless to say, there were many serious accidents over the years. Ollie Matheson particularly remembered the 1926 race. Ten riders were competing, jostling for position at the crest of the ridge. "A few of us decided to hold back," she recalled. She had decided well. The horses tangled up with each other on the narrow trail. "Half of them fell, rolling on top of one another. One horse broke its neck and had to be shot, others were badly injured, as were several riders who were hospitalized with bruises and broken bones. I was just happy to come in with my horse on its feet." After that disastrous year, Stampede organizers limited the number of entries to eight and eventually six. Rugged Alkali Lake cowboy Pierro Squinahan, who won the gruelling event eight times, was one of the riders injured in the 1926 fiasco. Squinahan carried the scars of that race for the rest of his life but was undeterred and rode in the race many more times.

Another interesting event at the Williams Lake Stampede in the 1920s was the attack on the "fort," a rough lumber enclosure constructed for the occasion.

Hans Richter (standing on his horse at the left) and cowboys at the Penticton Rodeo, 1916. Richter was one of the first rodeo contractors, driving his bucking horses from one rodeo to the next.
Okanagan Archives Trust photo

The Native cowboys, whooping and hollering, would charge down the hill and attack the fort and set it on fire. They would capture a "maiden in distress" and haul her away, kicking and screaming for effect. The white cowboys would then ride into sight at breakneck speed and "rescue" her. Then everyone would retire to the Native encampment for refreshments and visiting.

As rodeos became more popular, enclosed arenas were constructed and some ranchers, like Hans Richter in the South Okanagan, would assemble a "bucking string" of half-wild horses that they would bring to rodeos. Announcers, using megaphones, would inform the audience about the cowboys and horses that were about to appear and large crowds would gather. Prize money increased and grew more attractive, so that many cowboys would spend their summers riding from one event to another. If they could win enough to keep themselves fed they would be content but they were really doing it for the sheer thrill of riding or roping in front of a crowd of spectators. Inevitably some of them began to rise to the top of the heap and actually make a reasonable living at it. In addition, they were regarded as heroes in the ranching community.

Rodeo Heroes

Rodeo was the sport of choice in the ranching country of British Columbia. Ranch cowboys would spend their days off practising their roping, or riding broncs or steers, with hopes of someday winning an event in the local rodeo. Prize money in the local rodeos did not amount to much, and was often barely enough to cover a cowboy's costs, but the prestige gained among his peers was worth more than money. Champion bronc riders or calf ropers were regarded as heroes, men larger than life, to the rank and file of ranch workers. Cow bosses were quick to give talented riders or ropers time off to compete because winning an event in the local rodeo was good publicity for the ranch that the cowboy worked for. In the frontier days of ranching in British Columbia, the stagecoach drivers sat at the pinnacle of society; in the 1920s and 1930s that honour went to the rodeo champions.

Leonard Palmantier

One well-known rodeo champion was Leonard Palmantier, who came to the Cariboo in 1919 from his home in Riverside, Washington, to break horses for the Gang Ranch. He was a working cowboy for many of the big ranches, including the Douglas Lake, Gang and Alkali Lake ranches, but his first love was rodeo. Palmantier was one of the best bareback bronc riders around in the 1920s, consistently winning that event at the Williams Lake Stampede. In the early 1920s, after winning the bareback championship, he made an exhibition ride on one of the meanest bucking horses at the Stampede. Just to showcase his incredible skill, Palmantier decided to ride facing backwards. He stayed tight on the horse's back and spurred the whole time, riding the bronc to a standstill. He was "Best All-Around Cowboy in British Columbia" one year and, never one to lack showmanship, rode his horse into the Stampede Hall to claim his prize.

Palmantier married Josephine Grambush in 1935 and settled down on a ranch at Riske Creek. The couple had seven children and, not surprisingly, three of them were excellent riders. George and Jack Palmantier continued in their father's footsteps, winning many trophies and buckles over the next few decades. George was the best rider in British Columbia and consistently qualified for the North American Rodeo Championship finals, and Jack won the saddle bronc event at the national finals in Oklahoma City. Not to be outdone, their sister Joan, a barrel racer, was the Williams Lake Stampede Queen, BC Indian Princess and the Canadian National Indian Princess.

When Leonard Palmantier passed away in 1963, Eric Collier wrote this tribute:

Although almost 75 years of age and of failing health, Palmantier was riding for Mel Moon on fall roundup. On Monday, October 21st, he herded a bunch of yearling steers in off the range and put them into a pasture two miles from Allison's Store at Riske Creek. He then dropped in on us for a bit of lunch. A cold wind was keening in from the south east, bringing with it a mixture of sleet and rain. There was a deathly pallor on his face as he crouched over the stove, coaxing some warmth into his bones. He ate lunch with us, rolled a cigarette, sat around for a spell, discoursing on that one subject to which his entire mature life had been dedicated—range cattle. And listening to him I could not help but think: "He's no business being out punching cattle on a day like this." Then he thanked us for the tea, went outside, led his horse to a block of wood and hoisted stiffly into the saddle. And watching him ride away I thought; "But that's the way he wants it to be. He'll be riding and working cattle as long as he's sufficient strength to climb on a horse. Because it's the only life he knows, the only life he really cares for, the only one at which he's really happy." Twenty-four hours later, at his home at Riske Creek, Palmantier suffered a severe haemorrhage and was rushed to War Memorial Hospital, Williams Lake where . . . he serenely passed away on the forenoon of Thursday, October 24th.[6]

Carl "Slim" Dorin

Slim Dorin was a working cowboy, rodeo competitor and cow boss. He was born in the Wetaskiwin area of Alberta in 1913 and by the time he was 14 he was working as a teamster on a threshing crew. He moved to British Columbia in the 1930s and worked at the Douglas Lake Ranch and the Guichon Cattle Company as a bronc buster. Before long he was recognized as the legitimate successor to Bill Arnold as the best in the province at breaking horses. The "passing of the torch" from Arnold to Dorin took place one morning in spring when the range horses were driven into the corrals for the cowboys to pick their string of horses. Bill Arnold, then in his 70s, pointed out a little bay mare that he wanted to ride. But as soon as the cinch was put on her, it became quite evident that she was a time bomb waiting to explode. Slim saw that Arnold might have a time on this "snorty" horse and gently suggested that he "take the rough edge off her." Arnold smiled, knowing that his time at the top of the bronc-riding heap was past, and agreed that Dorin should ride her. Sure enough, the mare put on a real show and gave Dorin an opportunity to show his talent for sticking on a horse. After a hard ride, Dorin jumped off and suggested that they take the mare to cow camp and ride her a bit. Arnold thanked him but said he could handle her from there and jumped up in the saddle and rode off. The incident showed the mutual respect between the two men who made their living riding broncs.[7]

Slim's first love was rodeo and he competed in calf roping, saddle bronc, steer wrestling and

Leonard Palmantier was one of the best bareback riders in the province in the 1920s. He cowboyed for many of the big ranches, including the Gang, Alkali Lake and the Douglas Lake. *Museum of the Cariboo Chilcotin, Williams Lake photo*

Bill Arnold with Douglas Lake Ranch's stallion the Boss. At one time, Arnold was considered the best horse breaker in British Columbia. *Doug Cox photo*

team roping. He soon gained a reputation as one of the premier bronc riders in the province. In 1945, after the death of Joe Coutlee, he took over as cow boss at Douglas Lake Ranch, making him only the third man to occupy the position since the founding of the ranch in 1884. Slim moved in 1949 to take on the job of cow boss at the Nicola Stock Farm and, three years later, won the title of "All-Around Cowboy" at the BC rodeo finals. Slim also helped rodeos such as Merritt, Cloverdale and Williams Lake achieve their professional status. In 1952 he started as field man for the Cariboo Cattlemen's Association in Williams Lake and, in 1959, became head buyer in BC for Canada Packers. He retired in 1973.

Andy Manuel

Andy Manuel, one of Manuel Jovial's three sons, was born around 1887 and grew up on the Kamloops Indian Reserve. It was common at that time for Native children to take their father's first name as their last name. Andy was raised around horses and rode from an early age; when he was a young boy, his father was killed while chasing horses. Horses continued to play a major role in Andy's life. He spent some time as a Native constable and competed in the very first Calgary Stampede in 1912, as well as other rodeos all over the West. Between rodeos, Andy also worked as a cowboy for many of the ranches in the Kamloops area, including the Harper Ranch, Seven O and Lloyd Creek (Piva). When he was finished with rodeo, he started raising horses for riding and packing and also supplied horses for rodeo bucking stock. In the early days of rodeo, the only way to get horses to rodeos was to drive them overland. He even drove horses over the Coquihalla Trail to rodeos as far away as Vancouver. The story is told that it took two weeks to get the horses to Vancouver but two months to get them back home as Andy, flush with his stock contractor's wages, would visit friends all along the way. The first Falkland Stampede, which started out as a community picnic in 1919, where Cariboo cowboy Chris English attempted unsuccessfully to ride one of the local broncs, used Andy's bucking horses in the early years. Andy was the pride of the Shuswap people for his rodeo successes and there is even a lake behind Mount Lolo on the Kamloops Reserve named Andy Lake in his honour. During the Second World War, Andy and his son-in-law, Gus Gottfriedson, broke horses for the Canadian Army.

Merritt Stampede, 1935. Bronc riding was the favourite event among the spectators at early rodeos. *Historic O'Keefe Ranch photo*

Joe Elkins

Joe Elkins was born in 1903, the son of Edmund Elkins, the first white man in the Nemiah Valley, and a Tsilhqot'in Native woman. Joe's father ran a trading post in the remote valley but left his family after his brother Lewis, who ran another trading post near Tatla Lake, was murdered. Joe was adopted by Alex Humm, the brother of the murderer, and was raised on the Anaham Reserve. In 1916 he married Matilda Long Johnny and they lived in a small house on the reserve. They eventually owned a small ranch at Halfway Meadow north east of Alexis Creek, where Joe had a small herd of cattle and numerous horses. He put up as much as 250 tons of hay and wintered stock for other ranches. Joe and Matilda raised a family of 15 children and always managed to provide for their family, even in the toughest of times. For a few years in the 1930s he was ranch manager for the Anaham Reserve.

Joe loved rodeo and entered whenever he could, but the trip to Williams Lake for the Stampede took three to four days by team and wagon. He was a top bronc rider and won the bronc-riding competition at Williams Lake in 1929 and in 1949 and also won the Mountain Race at the Stampede. In 1964, at the age of 60, he successfully rode what was considered the meanest horse at the Stampede and he once rode a steer out of the chute backwards. Joe passed away in Quesnel in 1977.

Guest Ranches

With the coming of the motor car, the smaller stopping houses along the major roads in the Interior fell into hard times. No longer were travellers limited to 15 or 20 miles a day, which was about the distance that a horse and wagon could comfortably travel. This meant that the roadhouses that had served travellers for 60 years or more were forced to look for other means of income. Ironically, their opportunity also lay in motorized transport. With travel becoming easier, the first wave of tourists, people who actually travelled just to see new country, appeared in the Interior. Families could travel with all the food and belongings that they needed and enjoy the scenery. City dwellers could come to the beautiful Interior and fish in the multitude of lakes and hunt in the forests. At first, these tourists were looked upon as a nuisance, driving across private land and scaring the cattle. But, before long, enterprising ranchers started to see some potential for earning revenue to offset their losses from the lack of roadhouse traffic.

Big Bar Lake Guest Ranch and Fishing Camp

Such was the experience of Peg Marriott, whose husband, Harry, ran the OK Ranch near Big Bar on Big Bar Creek east of the Fraser River. She related:

> One day we came down, Harry and I, and we found people camped right beside the cabin. Harry was most annoyed and he told them to move off, that they had miles of land to camp in. Why did they have to camp right next to his little cabin? And they said that they felt safer . . . [Harry] went off in a huff because someone else's dog was chasing his spayed heifers. And I heard the American say something about "stupid Canadians" something like "ignorant Canadians, got a gold mine under their nose and don't know it." Well "a gold mine." That made me pick up my ears; after all, there was not a lot of gold in Harry Marriott's family. There were hardly any pennies in those days. So I go up to him and say, "What do you mean there's a gold mine under your nose? Where's the gold mine?" "Oh" he said "You could have a camp and some boats. You could have lots of people come. You could have lots of Americans if you had some boats and a few cabins." So after the man left and I came home, I said, "Harry, why don't we start one of those places where you rent boats?" Harry said, "I've got no money for boats." I said, "I could get some money for some boats." Oh he wasn't going to have any people on his place. He was an Englishman, his place was his castle. Everybody could stay outside his fence. But I thought "Oh these pennies, if I could have some of these golden pennies. So I worked on him and he finally gave me $300 and I bought five boats. They were made locally in Clinton. Each must have weighed half a ton. They were made of spruce   one inch boards. However, I had a start. Ronnie and I would come down here in the summer. Mostly Americans would come and Harry put me up one cabin. Wasn't long before the American fishermen would come and say, "Lady, we hate cooking! How about you doing our cooking for us?" Well I saw what they had in their grub box—beautiful fruits. In those days we didn't have savals [sic]. And to see these fruits, beautiful oranges and bananas and grapefruit and watermelons. Clinton never saw anything like that in those days. And I said, "Well I'll cook for you if you let Ronnie and I eat with you." Well that was just fine and that's how we started. And then they said, "Put up more cabins." And I said, "Well what do you charge people for things like this?" They said, "Charge a dollar a day for the boats and a dollar per cabin." And that was the start.[8]

Peg saw that the lack of refrigeration meant that their guests couldn't keep the lovely fish that they had caught. She convinced Harry to clean the snow off Big Bar Lake so he could cut blocks of ice, about 20 inches square, with an ice saw. The blocks would be slid onto a sleigh and hauled off the lake to a little shed in a shady corner of the ranch where they were covered with sawdust. With the sawdust insulation, the ice kept all summer long, to the delight of the fishermen. Peg Marriott was still running the Big Bar Lake Guest Ranch and Fishing Camp in 1952 when a fire swept through the camp and destroyed most of the buildings. Undeterred, Peg rebuilt the camp and continued to operate it, providing opportunities to fish, ride horseback, swim or just relax beside the lake for another 30 years. In 1980 she sold all but a five-acre lot that she lived on full-time until 1997 and in the summers until 2002. Harry Marriott died in 1979 but Peg lived until 2008 when she passed away just short of her 108th birthday.

TH Guest Ranch

The TH Ranch, named for its founder Orlando Thomas "Tom" Hance who first settled in the heart of the Chilcotin River valley in the 1860s, was also developed into a guest ranch. Tom's sons, Grover, Percy, Judd and Rene, inherited the ranch after their father's death in 1910. Unfortunately the ranch was deeply mired in debt from land and death taxes and Tom's widow, Nellie, refused to pay them until the government acknowledged the public road that Tom had constructed through the Chilcotin bush. Things appeared to be at a standoff and, for 15 years, the land taxes accumulated. Finally, in the mid-1920s, Rene Hance went to Victoria armed with documents and the support of local politicians to attempt to resolve the situation. After the minister of public works refused to see him, Rene went right to the top and met with Premier John Oliver to make his case. The premier agreed to cancel all the taxes owing in return for the cost of the road, thus freeing up the TH Ranch for the boys. Rene convinced his brother Percy, a returned First World War veteran, to join him and the two eventually purchased their brother Grover's portion of the ranch, the fourth brother, Judd, having died of pneumonia at a young age. The TH Guest Ranch was born. Percy and Rene were outgoing and charming hosts and the guest ranch prospered under their care until it was finally sold in 1966. The next year, Percy Hance died at the age of 74. His obituary in the *Calgary Herald* gave a glowing account of his and his brother's characters: "Percy was a delight to know. His sense of humour, soft spoken voice and gentle manner belied the kind of life he had led, for being a cowboy in the Chilcotin was anything but a soft life at even the best

Accommodations at the TH Guest Ranch. The ranch was founded by Thomas Hance in the 1860s and his sons, Percy and Rene, opened it to guests in the 1920s. *Museum of the Cariboo Chilcotin, Williams Lake photo*

of times. Hospitality was second nature to Percy and his brother, Rene, and the TH Ranch in the Chilcotin Valley is known all over Canada for just that old fashioned quality. People came back year after year—often times driving many miles out of their way across an impossible road—just to say hello to Percy and Rene."[9] The TH Guest Ranch changed hands after it was sold and eventually was subdivided into small holdings.

Grover Hance

No guest ranch would be complete without an authentic cowboy. Although Grover Hance was not involved in the operation of the TH Guest Ranch, he still lived there and, as he dressed and acted every inch the cowboy, was a colourful addition to the ranch experience. Grover Orlando Hance, the oldest son of Tom Hance, was a cowboy from the tips of his cowboy boots to the crown of his cowboy hat. He was a big, good-looking man who dressed carefully with a view to producing the greatest effect. He inevitably wore spurs with big rowels on his boots, a bright red bandana around his neck and angora chaps. Because of his authentic cowboy dress, he was by far the most photographed of the Hance brothers. But Grover did not just look like a cowboy. He was also an expert rider and roper and excelled at blacksmithing as well as leather and silver work, all traditional cowboy skills. His years on the cattle ranges and in the backcountry taught him a lot of rough and ready first aid, so he was enlisted whenever one of the cowboys or their family members had an accident. His brother Percy acknowledged his sometimes unorthodox treatments when he commented, "Grover's kind of a doctor."

Grover married Mary Wright in 1917 and the two chose to live off the TH Ranch. Instead, they lived on a meadow that Grover pre-empted on the south side of the Chilcotin River near Big Creek. Mary Hance died from tuberculosis in 1932. In the late 1930s, Grover married his second wife, Frances. The couple ran a guiding company in the Big Creek area east of the ranch. Grover eventually sold his share of the TH Ranch to his brothers but he and his wife lived in a small house there until Grover sold the house and property in 1960. His colourful dress and cowboy ways endeared him to TH Ranch visitors.

Grover's outspoken manner was balanced by his gentlemanly demeanour but occasionally his temper got the better of him. Woe betide any motorists who chose to honk their horn as they drove through Hance's spooky steers being driven down the road to the Williams Lake stockyards. They were subjected to a tirade of abuse that would make a sailor blush. On one occasion, when one of his hunting guides got a little carried away in his alcohol-infused enthusiasm, Grover neatly roped him and tied him to a Jack pine tree until he sobered up and promised to behave.

Ever the cowboy, Grover was feeding grain to his saddle horses at the age of 72 when he had an accident and broke his pelvis. He died at the Cariboo Memorial Hospital in Williams Lake of complications from the accident.

The Cornish Ranch and Three Bar Guest Ranch

Cornishman John Pollard pre-empted land in the Cut-Off Valley not far from Clinton in 1862. He established Pollard's Cornish Ranch and Roadhouse and ran a successful stopping house to serve travellers on the Cariboo Road, which had been constructed through his property. By the end of the First World War, Pollard's sons were still running the ranch but had seen business at the stopping place dwindle. They too saw opportunities in providing a ranch experience to the hundreds of travellers passing by on the road. The two Pollard sons, Tom and John Jr., agreed to split the property with Tom operating the cattle ranch and John starting up the Three Bar Guest Ranch, named after their cattle brand. Guests could experience life on a real cattle ranch while staying in the comfortable accommodation provided in the old stopping house. All summer long there was a steady stream of visitors through the old house, enjoying the beauty of the setting and the healthy ranch life. In the fall and early winter, John Pollard would guide hunters into the nearby hills where there were numerous moose and deer. John Pollard died in 1961 but his sons continued to operate the ranch as a hunting lodge until the 1980s.

Hi Huime Lake Fishing Camp

Budd Walters was born in Pittsburgh, Pennsylvania, but went to Texas at the age of 14 where he made his money breaking almost 400 horses for use in Yellowstone Park. He arrived in the Kamloops area in the early 1900s and worked breaking horses and driving the BX stagecoach. In 1920, he purchased the Circle W Ranch on Deadman Creek, west of Kamloops. His silent partner in the enterprise was an Englishman named Harry Devine who was well connected in Vancouver. At the upper end of Deadman Creek was Hi Huim Lake, which had an excellent reputation as a fishing lake, even though it was accessible only by saddle horse. It was so popular that the Pineapple King James Dole had paid the forest service to get a boat onto the lake for fishing. The forest rangers mounted the boat on a type of travois and a horse dragged it to the remote lake. In the early 1920s, Harry Devine asked Walters to take his secretary and a couple of friends up to the lake for some hunting and fishing. They were given permission to use Dole's boat and one of the lucky fishermen caught 100 fish. The fishermen persuaded Walters to open a fishing camp on the lake and make extra money by bringing in well-to-do clients.

As the Hi Huime Lake grazing area was on leased Crown land, Walters had to investigate whether he could open a fishing camp on the lake. He found out that, for $1 per cabin per year, he could lease the area. So, in the fall of 1926, he began to construct small cabins to house his hoped-for visitors. As there was still just a horse trail to the lake, he hired Native packers to bring in windows, doors and small cookstoves. By 1930, the Walters family had about 50 head of saddle horses bringing would-be fishermen to the lake. Finally, in 1942, Budd's son Jack Walters purchased a bulldozer and constructed a road to the lake.

Budd Walters' ranch continued to graze cattle at the far end of Deadman Creek and, during the winter, feed cattle from the haystacks. Jack Walters recounted the tale of feeding about 300 head of cattle and 100 head of horses during a particularly cold February when the temperature hovered around minus -60°F. He and two others were living in a cabin with a small box heater that simply could not keep up with the cold, so Walters suggested that they ride over to Hi Huime Lake and liberate one of the larger cookstoves from the cabins. It took the better part of a day, but the three men managed to make it to a cabin and light the cookstove before going to bed. They found that the cabins, built for summer use only, were freezing even with the cookstove roaring and they spent a fitful night sandwiched between slough hay and mattresses. In the morning, one of the cowboys, Slim Sutherland, decided to make hotcakes for the boys before they loaded up the stove and hauled it back to their cabin. He searched for baking powder for the hot cakes and, finding a jar of white powder behind the stove, he poured some in the batter. The resulting hotcakes were flat and Jack Walters commented that they were a little gritty. The other two men tasted the hotcakes and spit them out, deciding to skip breakfast that morning. It was some time later that they found out that the white powder in the jar had been Dutch Cleanser for cleaning the stoves.[10]

Pitchfork Artists and Stackers

By the 1920s, there wasn't a rancher in the British Columbia Interior who didn't feel the need to have large haystacks strategically placed on his ranch for winter feeding. Ranchers recognized that the amount of hay that a ranch could put up determined how many head of cattle could be wintered in a given area. Even though the occasional open winter would make hay redundant, the haystacks were their security and they seldom suffered the great "die-offs" that had occasionally devastated the cattle ranges in the early days. Haying was recognized as one of the necessities of ranching in the northern ranges and the routine of haying was as much a part of ranch life as branding and roundups.

Hay land was of two main types: natural meadows, or "wild hay," and cultivated hay land, or "tame hay." The natural meadows could be either valley bottoms or swamp meadows. The former were usually the flood plains of small streams that had a water table high enough to favour the growth of meadow grasses. The ranchers cleared such land of willows and other woody shrubs to make cutting the hay easier. In the spring, the land would be flooded naturally or the ranchers would build a crude earth dam at the lower end of the field to back up the water and perform flood irrigation. After the hay was cut in the summer, the cattle would be turned loose to graze on the land, just before winter feeding was started. Swamp meadows were usually in poorly drained depressions in the terrain that naturally collected water in the spring. Often the ranchers would have to dig ditches to drain the meadows prior to cutting the hay, usually in late June or early July.

Many ranches in the dry Interior, especially in the Thompson and Nicola regions, did not have enough wild hay lands to feed their cattle and had to grow their own tame hay. The most widely grown and most nutritious tame hay was alfalfa. A good crop of alfalfa was generally reckoned to produce up to two and a half tons per acre, whereas most mixed hays produced about half of that and wild hay about half again (about three-quarters of a ton per acre). Other tame hays included timothy mixed with clover, brome grass or red-top, all of which were considered to be more productive in higher elevations, where alfalfa was more susceptible to be killed off in the winter. Occasionally a cover crop of grain, usually oats, was planted before the alfalfa.

The primary form of providing irrigation water for tame hay was through ditches from creeks or lakes to the hayfields. There was a fine art to constructing an irrigation ditch. The grade had to be such that the water would carry any silt without filling in the ditch, and the water would not flow so fast that it would erode the bottom of the ditch. The Chinese excelled at digging irrigation ditches, having perfected their technique by digging ditches to bring water for hydraulic mining in the goldfields. It was said of the Chinese that "they were the only people who could make water run uphill." Harry Marriott described the process for determining if the lay of the land would allow for ditching when he was looking for land in the Big Bar area, just east of the Fraser River:

> I rode up to the Big Bar Lake again on a Sunday in early June of 1919 and I borrowed a good carpenter's level from my good friend Harry Coldwell, of Jesmond, and riding to the creek, I got off my horse and started taking sights along the level. This made me real sure that there was about ten to twelve feet of a fall in the mile or so distance from the creek to the flat—and that would mean I could take an irrigation ditch from the creek and run it out on to the main flat for irrigation . . . An irrigation ditch should have a smooth even-gaited flow if you want to get the best, and a fall of eight feet to the mile, or one quarter inch to every twelve feet is just about right for a good irrigation ditch.[11]

There were several approved methods to ensure that the drop of the ditch was uniform. Gordon Pooley, whose father started the Pooley Ranch in the Nicola Valley, told how his father taught him to survey ditches.

> To survey a ditch for ditch irrigation one uses two sticks, one six inches longer than the other, and a small hand held level, and two people. Start at the water source or lake and the person with the shorter stick walks off twenty paces from the person holding the level. The person with the level puts it on the top of the stick and sights the person twenty five paces away, who goes up and down the hill till he reaches a level sighting. At that point

he puts a stake in the ground to indicate the course of the ditch. That will give the ditch a six inch drop in twenty five paces, which will never erode or silt in.[12]

Another method of calculating the drop in an irrigation ditch was to make a wooden triangle and cut an inch off one side so that one side of triangle was longer than other. Then a plumb bob would be hung from the top. One man would hold the triangle and sight to another man up to 20 feet away, who would pound a stick into the desired location at the right height. Both of these methods provided a gradient that would allow the water to flow evenly and at the right angle. Where gulches or ravines could not be circumvented, flumes had to be constructed using the same grade to allow water flow.

Work on the hayfields would begin with the melting of the snow in March or April, when wild ducks would appear in every lake and puddle, a sure sign that spring had come. The swamp grasses that provided wild hay for ranchers would start to green up and would need little to no attention. For ranchers who supplemented their wild hay with seeded hayfields, it was time to work up the fields by ploughing up, disking, harrowing and reseeding the soil to tame grasses and legumes. All field work was done with horses.

In the spring, ditches would have to be prepared for use. Gordon Parke, whose great uncle had founded the Bonaparte Ranch near Cache Creek in the 1860s, told of the usual spring routine on the ranch.

The first job after the calves were born . . . was about 2 weeks of cleaning ditches, which my father insisted on and we cleaned that ditch that my great-granduncle had built. It was very, very hard work and it was all done with a shovel and you did it every day. You took your lunch with you and you went up into the ditch and you shovelled that ditch. You cleaned all the muck that had accumulated from the year before and the grass that had grown in. After the ditches were cleaned and the water was in the ditch, which was usually around the 20th of April, then we started moving cattle around and getting them out onto spring range.[13]

The Douglas Lake Ranch would employ up to 20 Chinese irrigators to look after the ranch's extensive hay lands. They would burn off the grass in the ditches and then clean them out so the water could be turned into the ditches. The ranchers who had built dams to flood their hayfields usually opened the dams up around July 1st. This gave the meadows about a month to dry out and gave the hay time to reach its optimum growth. And then it was haying time.

The earliest method of cutting hay was with scythes. This laborious process was still common in the earliest years of the 20th century. George Batstone, who settled in the Nicola Valley, remembered his first experience with a scythe.

> Three of us had a job haying at Thynnes. Of course none of us had ever worked at haying before, but we were all young and strong and soon learned. I remember an old timer that worked there and I was sent with him to scythe hay. He didn't know I just came from Boston and never saw a scythe before, and when he saw me cutting just the tops off he said, "Cut it close to the stubble, my boy." I never forgot or forgave him for teaching me how to use that scythe! We surely earned our $1.00 a day and board and we slept in the hay loft. Someone had a pair of clippers and we all had our hair clipped. We sure made a mistake as the mosquitoes were very bad, and we had to keep our heads under the blankets at night. When you were in the brush patches scything and cut right into a hornets' nest no matter which way you ran the hornets would be there ahead of you. We were sure sorry we clipped our hair![14]

After the hay was cut with a scythe it was raked by hand into bunches or "hay cocks," which were topped off to shed the rain. These were pitched by fork onto a wagon and hauled to the barn or haystack.

Although scythes were still used in wet areas where a horse-drawn mower might bog down, in most places, they soon gave way to horse-drawn mowers. When they were first harnessed up for haying, even the most experienced horses would be frisky after being out to pasture for the first time since the springtime work had been completed. Training young horses to pull the mower could also be challenging. The ominous whirring behind their heels made many of them nervous, jumpy and difficult to control. Only the best teamsters were put on the mowers and first-time colts were always teamed with an experienced, gentle horse. Colts began their training as three- or four-year-olds but by then, especially at the Douglas Lake Ranch where Clydesdales were used, they could weigh between 1,500 and 1,800 pounds. Workhorses never reached their prime until they were at least seven years old. At the beginning of haying, the teamster would be careful not to work the colt too much, usually trading one colt for another at noon. Even then, there were runaways. Often, two horses would appear in the yard with only the frame of a mower, the cutting bar and wheels having been lost as the runaways careened through the rough country.

Mowing could only be done once the morning dew had dried because damp grass jammed the mower knife. Warm dry days were required and ranchers watched the weather constantly during haying. Once mowed, the hay lay in the swath for about two days to cure in ideal conditions of warm sunshine and brisk breezes. This would reduce the hay's moisture content enough for it to be stacked, and every rancher had his own way of estimating the moisture level. Some twisted the hay into a rope to see if it would break; others felt the hay on the ground or chewed the stems.

Once the hay was considered dry enough, the simplest method of gathering cured hay was to rake it into piles with a dump rake. This rake, usually 10 feet wide, had a set of long, curved tines mounted on a frame set between two large wheels. Dump rakes had become standardized by the 1890s and remained virtually unchanged until the 1950s. An operator sat on a seat mounted above the frame, working a lever to lift the rake teeth when they were full. Normally he had only a single horse to handle, but a team could be used for heavy hay. Usually by raking time any initial friskiness was gone and the horses had settled down to business and plodded steadily along. It was then that the pitchfork came into play.

The loose hay was pitchforked directly onto hay wagons or "hay sloops" pulled by a team of horses. A novice pitcher soon learned the importance of pitching upwind of the wagon or sloop, as the dust and seeds would blow right into a pitcher's face if he was downwind. In the hay meadows of British Columbia, hay sloops were very popular for loading hay. These "sloops" consisted of two sleigh-type poles for runners with a deck made of poles like a stoneboat. Sloops were preferred in many places as they were low to the ground and easier to load. Pitching the hay onto stacks entirely by pitchfork limited the height that a stack could reach but meant that the entire process of haying could be accomplished with a minimum of equipment. Most ranchers preferred to use hay slings so that they could build large haystacks, so they designed their wagons or sloops to hold the slings. In front they had two four-foot uprights and a crosspiece to hold the ring at the end of the hay sling. Cables ran from the front ring along the sides of the sloop or wagon and then in to a second ring at the front of a second sling. The second sling was built the same way as the first, except it had a trip ring with a short rope attached to it. Before loading, the slings were spread out and hooked together on the sloop or wagon.

Once the hay was pitched onto the deck of the sloop or wagon, the load was pulled to the haystack and a rope was attached to the rings of the hay sling at either end. The entire load could then be lifted by a pulley to the top of the haystack by the team of horses that had brought the load. The trip ring was then released and the hay dropped onto the stack.

Workhorses at the Hill Ranch near Osoyoos, 1915. The horses have leather netting over them to keep the flies off.
Okanagan Archives Trust photo

Bob Webb with a team mowing hay on the Kruger Ranch near Skaha Lake in the South Okanagan, 1930s. *Okanagan Archives Trust photo*

Instead of slings, some ranches used hay forks, with three-foot-long prongs that opened and then closed onto the hay, to grab the hay off the wagons or sloops. When the prongs were driven down into the hay as deep as possible, a lever at the top was activated to turn the end three inches of the fork at right angles to the prong. This held the hay on the fork as a horse pulled the load by means of a pulley up to the top of the stack. Then the stacker would holler, "Dump!" and the driver of the horse would pull a rope and trip the fork, causing it to open and drop its load.

As the techniques for haying advanced, many large ranches purchased or constructed their own hay sweeps or, as they were often called, "bull rakes," to bring the hay to the stacks. When viewed from the top, a horse-driven sweep was shaped like a large "A." The horizontal bar of the "A" had 8 to 12 long poles or "teeth" extending from the front and lying flat on the ground. Behind the teeth was a three-foot-high fence that sat overtop an axle and two wheels set near the outside. At the back of the sweep (the point of the "A") was the driver and, directly in front of him and behind the fence, a team of horses. The driver would pull a lever to raise the front of the teeth a few inches. This ingenious device allowed a good teamster to push the sweep down a windrow of hay and then lift it up and carry it to the stack. There, just

Haying at Clarke Ranch, north of Williams Lake. Before the use of hay slings became common, all of the hay was moved by pitchfork. *Museum of the Cariboo Chilcotin, Williams Lake photo*

Hay sloop on the Kruger Ranch, 1930s. The hay sloop was little more than a deck sitting on two pole runners that slid along the ground. *Okanagan Archives Trust photo*

Stacking hay at the Chilco Ranch, 1920s. Hay was piled onto the sloops on top of hay slings that could lift the entire load to the top of the haystack. *Museum of the Cariboo Chilcotin, Williams Lake photo*

under a ton of hay at a time was set down on hay slings that could be attached to the hook and lifted up by a pulley arrangement onto the stack.

Various types of stackers were developed to get the hay from the ground to the top of the stack. The boom stacker consisted of a long horizontal pole, or boom, with pulleys on either end that swivelled on top of an upright pole. A rope ran through the pulleys and one end of the rope had a hook to fasten to the hay sling. Once the sling was hooked, a horse would pull the other end of the rope and raise the hay load to the top of the boom, where it was swung over the haystack and released, dropping the hay onto the top of the stack. The rope was then pulled back, ready to hook to another load of hay. After hay sweeps became common, the overshot stacker was developed and the hay slings were no longer necessary. The sweep loaded the hay onto the stacker, which had teeth that matched the sweep. The teeth were mounted on one end of a crossbeam that could be raised by the same team of horses via pulleys at each end until it reached the top of the poles, where it was flipped over onto the haystack. Various other stackers were used in the Interior, with each "expert" convinced that his version was the best.

Every rancher kept his eye on the clouds in the west during haying, for rain could spoil hay and significantly slow down progress. Wet hay in the stack was not only prone to rot, but, even more frightening, was also susceptible to spontaneous combustion. Many a stack or barn was lost through wet hay. A certain amount of moisture could be tolerated and ranchers found that coarse salt spread liberally on the hay as it was stacked would draw out the moisture and dry out the hay. The salt was cheap to purchase and easily obtained and was so effective that even the wettest hay would cure and be used as feed through the winter.

There was a definite class system among the haying crew. The stacker, responsible for building a uniform stack that could shed water, was at the top of the haying hierarchy. Stacks that were not built properly and allowed moisture to get into the centre ended up as solid ice in the winter with the hay all knotted together. It would take a great deal of effort to saw and chop the hay to get it on the load in sub-zero weather. A good stacker would "top off" the haystack so that it was shaped like a loaf of bread, high in the middle and tapered on the sides and ends so that it could shed water. Stackers not only carried a great deal of responsibility but also lived with an element of danger in their work. In the South Okanagan, one of the hazards for the stacker was rattlesnakes! The snakes would be hidden in the rows of cut hay and be

Team of Clydesdales on a hay sweep, Douglas Lake Ranch. Hay sweeps eliminated the need for loading the hay with pitchforks. *Doug Cox photo*

picked up with the hay sweep. When the hay was picked up and dropped onto the top of the stack, the snakes would be revealed and would be quite cranky. Stackers had to be quick with a pitchfork to throw them off the stack or there could be serious consequences.

If the stacker was the top man on the haying crew, the derrick man, who had the monotonous task of driving the horse that pulled the hay up to the top of the stack all day long, was at the bottom. In between were the teamsters and hay pitchers, who took great pride in their skill. Mower men were careful to cut every bit of hay right up to the edge of the irrigation ditches and not to leave a blade of grass standing. Rakers made sure there was no hay left in the field when they were done and were careful not to drag the hay too far and knock leaves off the precious hay. Teamsters on the wagons or sloops made sure that the load was built evenly and squarely. Pitchers made sure that the hay cock was solidly placed on the deck. A poorly built load might come apart on the way to the stack or when it was lifted up onto the stack. A well-built load could be lifted in even loads up the stack without causing the stacker to waste a lot of effort spreading them out.

Experienced teamsters employed many labour-saving tricks. They manoeuvred carefully so that they could load their wagon or sloop going downhill so the horses would have an easy start to pull the full load back to the stack. They also worked at building their load in the direction of the haystack so that, once loaded, the horses had the shortest distance to pull it.

Even though haying took place in the hottest days of summer, when mosquitoes and hornets could make life miserable, most

Chilco Ranch haying crew, 1920s. Natives made up a majority of the workers employed on haying crews throughout the BC Interior.
Museum of the Cariboo Chilcotin, Williams Lake photo

workers enjoyed the work. Haying crews swelled the ranks of employees at the ranches and put pressure on accommodations, so the first few loads of fresh hay that were loaded went right to the barn where they would be put into the hayloft. The majority of the crew would stay there during haying, sleeping in the hay. After long, hard days in the summer sun, it certainly gave meaning to the term "hit the hay." The crew would be fed at the ranch house and food was plentiful and tasty as the ranch women outdid themselves in preparing

meals for the starving crew. The crew in the hayloft "bunkhouse" had little leisure time for socializing but, for those with a propensity for gambling, there was always time for a game of chance and men were known to lose a whole day's wages in an evening. Nonetheless, everyone thought of haying as the big social event of the summer.

Edith Whiteford Currie, who grew up on the Tamerton Ranch owned by her father John Whiteford, remembered haying time with fondness:

> Haying times were wonderful, happy times. The dinner bell went at 6:00 a.m., 12:00 noon, and 6:00 p.m. The men were allowed an hour at noon, and they brought their horses in to water them, fed them and gave them a rest. The cook house was the summer kitchen. There were three tables in the kitchen dining hall. The Native men sat at the first table, the second table were the part Native, who didn't want to acknowledge their heritage, and white field hands, the third table was where the family ate. On looking back I don't think there was any class distinction, the Natives could talk their own language at the table and they felt more comfortable. They had a choice of eating at any table. In later years when all hands could speak English there was one table.[15]

Once the hay was all in, cattle were turned out on the hay lands to graze what was left until the winter snow made grazing impossible. In some localities such as the eastern edge of the Cariboo ranges, cattle were fed hay for as much as six months of the year. In the lower elevations, some ranches could get by feeding their cattle for as short a time as two months. But, through most of the Interior, ranchers considered themselves lucky if they could get by feeding their cattle hay for four or five months in the winter. In every case, the fear of that 1 bad winter in 10 kept the ranchers diligently haying and putting up enough hay to allow for even the longest winter.

Growing Up on the Ranches

It was the dead of winter on December 24, 1924, when the family of Cyrus and Phyllis Bryant arrived at the land Cyrus had pre-empted at Tatla Lake in the west Chilcotin. The children, Jane, Caroline, Alfred and Florence "Bunch," remembered arriving at this small log cabin and wondering what they were entering into. Bunch was only five years old at the time and, in this isolated location, her only playmates were her siblings. But her memories of growing up on her father's ranch illustrated that the hard, meagre existence on this remote pre-emption was far from difficult. She had a loving mother and father and, especially with her older brother Alfred, there was seldom a dull moment. She described one incident when she was nine.

Then Alfred and I decided we were going to learn to stand up and ride our horses, on the horse bareback with no saddle on. I saw him fall off 18 times in about 200 yards. We both learned to do it and were reasonably good at it. One time we were haying at the Alex Jack place, I guess it was, Alfred and I and daddy. Daddy was driving the team behind and of course Alfred and I had our saddle horses bareback. So, coming down this meadow toward home that night Alfred said, "See that white rock down there, Bunch? I'll race you to it standing up." I said, "Okay" and I turned to daddy and said, "You say go." He said, "You mutton-headed chumps, you're going to get killed one of these days. Alright, Go!" And away we went. Alfred's horse was a miserable little cuss and had a bad habit of, just when he started to run, he would stop and turn at right angles. Well that doesn't go very good for standing up and this is what he did. And Alfred, instead of falling flat, he landed running. I was ahead. My horse was faster anyway. I was looking back and laughing at him and suddenly my horse shied at the white rock. I'd reached it and hadn't realized and I landed flat on my stomach and just skidded like a sled. All the wind was knocked out of me and I can still see daddy coming down the meadow as fast as he could make the old horses trot, you know, and jumping down and picking me up and saying, "You mutton-headed chump. How many times are you going to scare your old pa to death?"[16]

Growing up on a ranch was not all fun and games, though. From the moment they could walk, most youngsters had chores to do every day of the week, from filling coal-oil lamps and cleaning lamp chimneys to helping with wash day. Children would be expected to help with gardening and to pick wild berries for canning. But, despite the never-ending routine of chores, ranches were a wonderful place to grow up.

Bunch Trudeau tells the story of a game that she and her siblings used to play. They always had a lot of books and the books enriched their lives. One of their favourites was *The White Company* by Sir Arthur Conan Doyle, set during the Hundred Years War. This story of knights and battles captured their imagination and transported them from the bush country of Tatla Lake to medieval England. The older children, Alfred and Jane, decided that they were going to be knights. Jane was usually Sir Nigel and Alfred was Richard the Lionheart. Alfred carved out a sword for each of them, and they would take poplar bark peeled from the tree and attach wires at the top and

Violet, Mel, Charlie, Dorothy and Rex "Pudge" Moon with surveyor Frank Swannell (with pipe) at the Deer Park Ranch. *Museum of the Cariboo Chilcotin, Williams Lake photo*

bottom so they could use it for a shield. Alfred didn't stop there; he made an entire suit of "armour" out of poplar bark—breast shield and arm and leg coverings. Caroline was always the damsel in distress and Bunch, the youngest, felt left out until Alfred generously said she could be his squire. Bunch was happy with that until she found out that squires couldn't ride horses and she wasn't allowed on a stick horse like the others. As if that wasn't bad enough, the squire had to carry the heavy poplar bark armour around for Alfred.

Bunch had some very special pets, ones that only a ranch kid would have had. The family was convinced that the surprise batch of kittens that their cat had birthed, without a tomcat in sight, was the result of a union with a mink. The surviving kitten had all the characteristics of its father and was totally attached to Bunch's father, Cyrus. It served as the family pet until it met an untimely demise, much to the dismay of the children. This most unusual family pet was succeeded by another unusual pet, but one that was a good deal larger:

Alfred came in one day and he had this little calf moose. He was awfully scrawny and he had brought it home thinking we could save its life and of course Caroline took it to her heart as she did every other little animal. And she went out and cut grass and we fed it and we fed it milk and the calf started to grow and she was doing splendidly. And she would follow her around; everywhere she went the calf would go. So it got to be quite a pet but it wasn't too bad. It stayed pretty much in its place. The only problem was you had to go out and cut grass for it because it wouldn't go out and feed by itself and it loved its milk. It couldn't drink milk standing up. It had to go down on its knees and drink its milk.

The family kept the moose calf, named Babs, and it weighed close to 200 pounds when the family moved to Anahim Lake. Getting the moose calf proved a challenge that Bunch and her sister Caroline were up to:

Caroline and I went down to get this calf just with saddle horses and we thought well we'd lead it up. It led about 11 miles then it decided that was enough and Babs laid down right in the middle of the road. Well we tried to get it up. We'd get it on its feed and it would lie down and just lay there and blatt . . . Well we just didn't know what to do. We were eight miles from the place where we were supposed to stay that night and I was riding kind of a half green animal. He was gentle enough but he wasn't very well broke. Caroline was riding a rather high spirited mare and we couldn't possibly load the moose on. So we decided we'd try one thing. We rode around the bend in the road and we sneaked back and had a look. When we got out of sight she got up but when she saw us Babs sat flopped down again. Well there was only one thing to do and that was to try and load that confounded moose on my horse. So we hoisted and we lifted and we struggled and at last got it part way up into the saddle with the front feet over and then one of us would run around to the other side and grab the front feet and we pulled and we pushed and we got her into the saddle and held her there until she stopped squirming. We tied her feet under the horse's belly and I rode behind the saddle . . . The next day, Jane came down with a wagon and she got the moose and hog tied it and she got it home.[17]

The Three "R"s

Educating children on the ranches was often difficult. If there was a large enough community to supply 10 children of school age the residents had to satisfy Victoria that there was title-deeded land for a school grounds. Once that was accomplished, a school board of three trustees had to be elected and then an application made to the department of education for approval.

The department would draw up the school district boundaries, which were subject to revision if the population shifted. There were two types of rural schools. The "assisted school" was built by the community at its own expense, usually with the help of volunteer labour. The government would then provide blackboards, desks and books and pay the teacher's salary. The second type was called a "regular school," which was constructed and equipped by the department of education, which paid two-thirds of the teacher's wage. The remaining third, as well as any other needs, had to be paid by the local residents. The department of education also supplied all schools with certain textbooks and a few teaching aids, such as chalk, a pointer, several maps and the strap, an ominous-looking 2-foot-by-1½-inch piece of rubber belting. The school board submitted an annual budget to Victoria and ensured that the teachers, and children doing janitorial work, were paid every month. The school board was also responsible for firewood and repairs.

The teachers were normally 18- and 19-year-olds who had just graduated from Normal School. They would often be chosen sight unseen from letters of application, a practice that could bring surprises on both sides. But, whenever possible, the school board would invite the prospective teacher to a face-to-face interview so they could better assess the candidate's suitability. One female teacher being interviewed by the Big Creek school board in the Chilcotin, on being informed that there was a tub that could be filled with water and heated on the school stove for baths, informed the board that she would rather wait for five months until she returned to Vancouver for her bath! Most young teachers had never been out of the city and few lasted more than a year. Those who did last had to be strict disciplinarians or engaging teachers as some of the pupils, especially the older boys, could be bigger and certainly tougher than the teacher. Teachers had to instruct grades one to eight and generally were responsible for organizing dances, picnics and the annual Christmas concert. They supervised ball games, settled arguments and applied first aid and sympathy. At times incredible sensitivity was required and often a straight face, as when a teacher was called on help extricate a mouse that had scampered up a hysterical 16-year-old's pants and through the fly of his long johns when he tried to stamp on it. The majority of school teachers were young women and they inevitably spent some of their time rebuffing the amorous advances of every young man in the district. Often there was one young man who succeeded where others had failed and there was many a rancher's wife who had started out as a "school marm."

While discipline was tight, sometimes things would turn out all right. George Turner from the Kleena Kleene Valley attended the little school at Tatla Lake that had been built next to the Bryants' house because they had the most children in the area. It was April 1st and George thought he would play an April Fool's joke on the teacher, Mr. Brown. That day the students had a spelling test where the paper was passed to the person ahead of them for correction and then given back to the student. Mr. Brown called out each student's name and they gave their results. When he got to George Turner, George called out, "All wrong . . . April Fool!" Mr. Brown was not impressed and told George to fetch the strap. With shaking hands George brought the strap forward and held out his hand. The teacher raised the strap with a menacing look in his eye and then gently set it down on George's trembling hand. "April Fool! Now go take it back."

School was not all studies and there was plenty of time for games. In the spring and fall, it was Pom-Pom-Pullaway, Prisoner's Base, Anti-Anti I Over and softball. Spring meant that the boys would bring out their marbles and the girls would scratch an area in the dirt where they could play hopscotch. Once winter snows covered the playing area, the students stayed inside close to the wood heater. A popular indoor game was Fox and Geese, played on a checker board where the fox checker tries to capture 13 geese checkers by jumping them before they surround him.

No matter what school you attended, some things were always the same: the two identical buildings out back marked "Boys" and "Girls," the barn where you could tie your saddle horse and the little (mostly log) schoolhouse. Every schoolhouse served as a community centre as well, hosting such diverse activities as political meetings, dances, performances, church services and young ranchers' meetings.

For children on the more isolated ranches, the government instituted the BC Correspondence Course whereby children could be educated at home. Jack Durrell, whose father owned the Wineglass Ranch in the Chilcotin, got his entire education up to grade eight by correspondence. The Wineglass was about 12 miles from the nearest school bus route, and in the winter the drive could take up to two hours, which was not really practical. Taking school by correspondence required discipline and it usually fell to the children's mother to shoulder that dubious responsibility. Each mom established her own routine and stuck with it. Jack Durrell reflected on that. "Every family set up their own system I guess. Mother tried to keep up regular school hours but us kids would make any excuse to get away from it. My wife did it differently. She had no formal strict hours. It might start at 7:30 in the morning and, if the day's assignment was done by 9:30 or 10:00, they were off for the day. Sometimes if they were old enough to go riding for a few days, they could go all right but then they would have to make it up with double time for a while."[18]

In a world where education was regarded as one of the most important aspects of a young person's upbringing, there was always an emphasis on giving children opportunities for learning away from school. Long before the 4H name was accepted, there were Boys and Girls Clubs in the ranching areas. Started in BC in 1912 with garden clubs, the movement eventually included swine, poultry and beef clubs. The first Boys and Girls Clubs were loosely organized and met only once or twice a year, with field days at various farms and ranches during the spring and summer. Members were taught the finer points of judging and animal care. Their projects were judged at home and sold privately. Members of the Beef Club south of Kamloops showed calves at the Kamloops Fall Fair and at the Bull Sale in March, where they showed and sold their animals. There were no records kept and no regulations as to the number of days the calves could be fed grain before showing. Ernie Haughton of the Beresford area south of Kamloops entered a "calf" in the Boys and Girls section of the 1929 Bull Sale that weighed in at 1,140 pounds and sold for 1¾ cents a pound!

Settling the Fringes

Kennon Beverly Moore was born in Boston to a family that traced its ancestors to the *Mayflower*. The pioneer blood must have run in his veins because in 1912, at the age of 21, he left his comfortable home for the Canadian West. He vowed to travel into the wilderness until he found a place where he could make a home for himself. His travels brought him to the Chilcotin where he worked for Norman Lee until he could get the lay of the land. Then, in the spring of 1914, he rode first west and then south into the remote valley of Tatlayoko Lake, where the lush spring grass grew. He knew immediately that he had found what he was looking for. But, before he could take up land, news of the war in Europe reached him and, even though his country was not yet embroiled in the conflict, he enlisted with the Royal Canadian Engineers. In 1917 he went overseas to France. His search for land would have to wait until the war was over. While in France, his unit was laying track for ammunition cars behind the lines when he and his company were gassed. He survived and, after recuperating in Scotland, headed back to Canada to chase his dream. The Tatlayoko was one of the only places in British Columbia where good land was still available, so he filed for a homestead at the north end of Tatlayoko Lake and began clearing land for a home. He used controlled burning to clear off the thick underbrush and blasting powder for the more difficult stumps. His home was taking shape and now his challenge was to find someone to share it with him. He travelled east along the dirt road that ran through the Chilcotin and, in 1920, courted and married Dora "Dolly" Church, daughter of pioneer settlers at Big Creek. Ken and Dolly began with little more than a garden patch and, through hard work and perseverance, cleared hayfields and began to raise Hereford cattle. The couple soon had two children, Beverly and Isabel, to raise on their remote ranch. The cattle drive to Williams Lake took a gruelling 20 days and, with the price of beef low, brought them only enough cash to buy a sack of flour. The struggle was too much for Dolly and, while Ken was on a beef drive, she packed up her belongings and their two children and left. But Ken persisted in following his dream. Despite setbacks and disappointment he continued to raise cattle and, in the fall, would guide hunting parties after grizzly bears. Ken's poverty did not discourage him from offering hospitality to any neighbour or stranger who passed by. His reputation for honesty and reliability was respected throughout the Chilcotin. Eventually his son and daughter returned to work with their father and Ken's lonely days were over. He stayed at Tatlayoko until 1953, when he was hospitalized in Vancouver for cancer treatment. He died there the following year, but his indomitable spirit and love of the land were remembered by all who knew him.

By the beginning of the 1920s, land for ranching was getting harder to find. Only the most inaccessible areas of the Cariboo and Chilcotin had any land available. The remote corners of these vast regions still had meadows that had never seen a cow and remained the province of deer and moose. But pioneers like Ken Moore were deterred by neither distance nor hardship as they opened up the remote corners of the province. Areas like Bradley Creek, Ruth Lake and Hawks Lake in the Cariboo and Anahim Lake and the Kleena Kleene in the Chilcotin were opened in the 1920s and other areas that had only seen a few settlers now began to attract homesteaders.

Tatla Lake was one of these areas. It had been settled as early as the 1890s by Lieutenant Joseph Martin, formerly of the Royal Navy and a member of the government team that surveyed the Chilcotin starting at Bute Inlet in 1890. According to the *Victoria Colonist*, Martin had developed a "fine ranch" there by the end of 1890. Martin sold out to Benjamin Franklin, who had previously established a dairy farm near Alexis Creek. Franklin hoped to prove the feasibility of constructing a road down the Klinakline River to Knight Inlet. He actually made the trip with two Native men in six days and then proceeded by water to Victoria. But the government was unimpressed and the project never went any further. Franklin sold out to Bob Graham in the early 1900s and a handful of other intrepid settlers trickled in over the next 20 years.

In the early 1920s there was still excellent land available at Tatla Lake for settlement. In 1924, Cyrus and Phyllis Bryant heard about this and set

Ranches in the remote wooded areas were often called "stump ranches"—and for good reason.
Historic O'Keefe Ranch photo

out from Soda Creek with their four young children to pre-empt land at Tatla Lake. By the time they loaded up two wagons with all their belongings and left Soda Creek, it was November and the snow was beginning to fall. One night, Mrs. Norman Lee of Lee's Corner invited them to spend the night at her place. Since they had been camping out in a tent since they left, they readily agreed, carefully placing a kerosene lantern under one of the wagons to keep their vegetables from freezing. During the night, the lantern set the wagon on fire and the entire load burned to the ground. Phyllis had brought her pride and joy, a piano, on that wagon and was heartbroken over the loss. But such were the vicissitudes of homesteading.

Another remote area of the Chilcotin was Chezacut, an area rich with natural meadows, but far off the beaten track. Again, settlers had come into the area in the early 1900s but, because of its isolation, there had been no rush for land. Frank Shillaker came to Chezacut in 1920 after serving in the First World War. He worked for various people in the area then purchased the Chezacut General Store in 1927, which he operated until 1970. In this remote area the general store was also the fur-trading post and Frank traded furs that the Native people had trapped in surrounding bush. He hauled all his freight over the 30-mile-long wagon track through Jack pine forest from Redstone to Chezacut, using a sleigh during the cold winter months. In spring he fought his way through incredible mudholes with his horse-drawn wagon so that he could pick up the mail and freight for his neighbours as well as his own necessities. Like all country stores,

Tatla Lake cowboys. At the end of cattle drives, cowboys would often spend their wages on new hats and blue jeans. *Museum of the Cariboo Chilcotin, Williams Lake photo*

the Chezacut General Store was the centre of the small community, where neighbours would meet and exchange news. When Frank sold out in 1970, he spent his winters with his wife, Ruby, in New Westminster. But the hustle and bustle of city life did not appeal to him and he would head back to his little cabin at Chezacut every spring. One fall, when a neighbour asked him, "Are you going home for the winter?" Frank replied, "No, I'm leaving home for the winter." His heart remained in the remote corner of the Chilcotin that had been his home for more than 50 years.

Dan Buys a Herd

Norman Lee had been in the Chilcotin since 1884 and the story of his epic cattle drive to the Klondike goldfields in 1898 was legendary. Setting out with 200 head of cattle in the spring, Lee had endured incredible hardships as he drove his cattle up the old Telegraph trail through Northern British Columbia. After reaching Teslin Lake on the Yukon border, Lee butchered his cattle and loaded the beef on rafts, hoping to get to Dawson City. But a fierce storm descended on them and broke up the rafts, sending the beef to the bottom of the lake. Undeterred, Norman Lee struggled back to the Chilcotin, penniless but not discouraged, to start all over again. Lee returned to England for a visit in 1902 and returned with a bride, Agnes, who, despite a genteel upbringing, found the rugged outdoor life of the Chilcotin to her liking. The Lees had no children, but they travelled to England in 1905 and adopted a three-year-old boy, Daniel. Dan turned out to be a Chilcotin character in his own right and his strong personality thrived in the rough-hewn life of the frontier.

Early in life, Dan's strong opinions asserted themselves. One day, at the age of six, he was out touring the area with a young woman whose enthusiasm for the Chilcotin was unbounded. "Isn't it beautiful?" she enthused as they viewed the scenic panorama, "Don't you just love it?" Without hesitation, Dan replied, "No. I've been here for three years and I'm sick of it." When Dan was sent to boarding school in Victoria, his apparent dislike for the Chilcotin changed to love. He returned home as a six-foot-four young man and took to the cowboy way of life with enthusiasm. By then his parents were operating a store and trading post as well as their ranch, but Dan was more interested in ranching than storekeeping. The problem was that he had no herd and no obvious likelihood of purchasing one.

In the summer of 1929, Dan was at his parents' store when a Native cattleman, Capoose, rode in with a sad story. He had 100 head of cattle at Anahim Lake and had wanted to sell them to Cousins Spencer, owner of the huge Chilco Ranch. But Spencer, a hard-headed businessman, had refused to pay what Capoose thought was a fair price. As Capoose shared his dejection, Dan thought to himself, "It's now or never." He asked Capoose to hold on to his cattle and made a hasty trip to Williams Lake where he pitched his idea to the local banker. The banker, sensing that the price of cattle was going to go up, agreed to loan Dan $5,000 to start up a herd. Dan returned home on cloud nine and closed the deal with Capoose, giving him $200 as a down payment. But that was just the beginning of Dan's buying spree. As he prepared to drive his new herd back from Anahim Lake, he let the word out that he was in market for any cattle available. And, in preparation for the added cattle, he spent a week putting together a camp and hiring two Native cowboys, Joseph Bobby and Edward Johnny. Dan's spending spree went on for three months as word got out that he was paying top dollar for cattle and was paying cash on the barrel. Ranchers from throughout the backcountry were eager to see some cash for a change and, everywhere Dan and his crew passed, ranchers would bring in a few head at a time for Dan to consider. In the ranching country, a man's word was as good as a contract and a handshake would confirm any deal, but Dan was nonetheless impressed when one of Capoose's Native cowboys rode for two days to return $200 to Dan that he had forgotten to subtract when he paid Capoose out. The cowboy rode up to Dan and grinned at him. "You make mistake," he said, handing Dan a roll of $200.

It was October before Dan got back to Lee's store, bringing with him a mixed herd of cattle, including an old steer that weighed in at a massive 1,760 pounds! It turned out that, as Dan had been wending his way through the Chilcotin, the price of cattle had been going up. He pushed on to Williams Lake where, much to his surprise, three cattle buyers were waiting for him, offering him nine cents to the pound, which meant that he was making around a $100 a head, one of the best prices in that decade. Dan sold off most of the herd, paid off his loan plus one that his father had incurred years before, and still had enough left to begin purchasing purebred Herefords. Soon his cattle commanded top price and Dan's tall figure became a fixture at the Williams Lake stock sales for the next 50 years.

The 1920s had been a decade of huge change in the ranching regions of British Columbia. The long drives to the railhead at Ashcroft were a thing of the past as ranchers in the Cariboo and Chilcotin could now drive their cattle to the nearest Pacific Great Eastern loading point. By the end of the decade, the motorized vehicle had taken the place of the horse-drawn wagon for road travel, except in winter where the sleigh was the only way to navigate unploughed roads. As well, the 1920s saw the first widespread use of purebred bulls for breeding and the practice of de-horning cattle as meat packers protested the damage and bruising caused by horns in shipment. Change had been especially significant in the Chilcotin. The only fences at the beginning of the decade had been the ones around winter pastures along the rivers and around a few quarter-section homesteads. By 1929, the Chilcotin ranges were almost entirely fenced and large-scale community roundups were uncommon. The price paid for Dan Lee's cattle in the fall of 1929 reflected the strong market for beef in the late 1920s when North America was riding the postwar boom. It seemed that prices would only continue to increase and that ranching would ride the wave of prosperity that the rest of society was enjoying. But October 29, 1929, signalled a time of drastic change in the world economy that would affect everything, including the ranching life.

Native cowboys from the Douglas Lake area. Ranches in the British Columbia interior depended upon the Native cowboys to supply much needed labour. *Historic O'Keefe Ranch photo*

Chapter Three

BUST YEARS

Dan Lee had been paid nine cents a pound for his cattle in October 1929 and had averaged $100 a head for mixed cattle of dubious lineage. But the stock market crash at the end of that month resulted in a steady drop in cattle prices, as the wages, industry and number of jobs shrank. As Harry Marriott remembered:

> In the fall of 1930, I came home from shipping my carload of beef cattle with a baby cheque of $531.45 for the whole twenty-five head, which was our whole year's output. The day the beef were shipped each year was looked forward to by all ranchers and cattlemen as being one of the most particular days of the year. That was the only pay day we had in a whole year that amounted to anything. In those depression years it became just a day of gloom and disappointment, because we knew that the whole beef cheque would only pay part of our expenses and debts, and that most of us were being further bogged down in the economic pot-hole.[1]

As the average income of people eating beef dropped, so did the demand for larger, more expensive cuts, causing packing houses to demand lighter cattle, from which smaller cuts could be made. During the 1930s, the market demanded more two-year-old steers, averaging 1,000 pounds, instead of the previous market for three-year-old steer averaging 1,200 pounds. This meant that ranchers would get less per animal, even though they would be able to sell them a year earlier.

Fred Nason and Ralph Newman, cowboys at the Beaver Ranch in the Nicola Valley. Both are wearing "wild rags," silk neckerchiefs that could filter out dust during cattle drives. *Historic O'Keefe Ranch photo*

By 1934, the beef market had bottomed out. Ranchers were lucky to get 2½ cents a pound for steers, 1½ cents for heifers and ¾ cent for cows. Alex Bulman tells of being offered 150 head of good range cows in the fall of 1934 for 1½ cents a pound and offering instead 1 cent a pound for the best 100 and ½ cent a pound for the remaining 50. The seller had little choice but to accept the offer, as he would not do better anywhere else. One old-time rancher was heard to remark about the rock-bottom prices of cattle, "When you go to figuring what an old cow brings these days, she don't hardly make a mark on the paper."[2]

As the flow of cash dwindled to a trickle, ranchers avoided paying cash as much as possible and preferred to trade goods whenever possible. In 1933, Frank Ward at the Douglas Lake Ranch exchanged three of his bulls for three belonging to a rancher in Squilax. In what must be considered one of the boldest proposed trades of all, a Vancouver realtor offered—albeit unsuccessfully—to exchange the Douglas Lake Ranch for a nine-storey office building in St. Paul, Minnesota. Another rancher was to write, "I have got lots of Alfalfa seed No. 1 and 2 or 300 boxes of Golden Russet apples, which I would like to trade for a bull 2 or 3 years old and a heavy young work horse trained to harness."[3]

Hardships and Challenges

Grasshoppers

Just when ranchers thought that things couldn't get any worse, nature also turned against them. The already dry Interior became even drier, shrinking pastures and hay crops. And grasshoppers arrived with a vengeance. These pests would hatch in the spring on the pasture lands, which they promptly ate out of existence. Then, having grown to about a quarter of an inch long, they would head for the hay and grain crops, which were just turning a promising green. The young grasshoppers were too small to hop the wider irrigation ditches and would fall in the water and drown, plugging the ditch solid. Irrigators would have to shovel the wet, decaying bodies out of the ditches to allow the water to flow through. Wet weather would slow down their growth but the 1930s brought little rain and the plague of grasshoppers worsened.

Edith Whiteford Currie, whose father owned the Tamerton Ranch in the Nicola Valley, described the situation: "The weather was dry and the grasshoppers were terrible. During the afternoon the clouds of these insects would fly to the lake, and would be two to three inches thick. The horses hated them, and we had to have a burlap strip to flap over their nose, tied to the nose band of the bridle to help the horse. Grass became scarce, and one year the cattle were forced to eat bull rushes at the end of the lake."[4]

As the situation grew worse, the district agriculturist in Kamloops came up with a formula that he thought might help. Aware that grasshoppers loved horse manure and salt, he developed a concoction of horse manure seasoned with a strong sprinkling of salt and laced with Paris Green (an oxide of copper) poison. The formula seemed to work for the grain farmers in particular. They could spread the mixture along the edges of their fields early in the morning so it would stay moist enough for the grasshoppers to eat it. Knowlton Lewis, whose father farmed south of Kamloops, reported, "Getting the manure was time-consuming; it meant going over the pasture every other day or so. A tub and shovel were carried any time a wagon or buggy left home. Even going to church on Sunday I rode 'shovel gun' with my feet hanging over the back of the buggy—when I heard 'Whoa' I was off with my bucket and spade."[5] The next year, arsenic was substituted for the Paris Green and proved to be even more effective. There is no record of the effect it had on the farmers and ranchers who soon came to treat the 10-pound cans of arsenic as though they contained flour.

Fortunately, the grasshoppers had their own natural enemies and disappeared after a three-year cycle. In the second year of the cycle, a red parasitic mite took its toll on them, and in the third year, a small wasp that laid its egg inside the grasshopper appeared. By fall of the third year of the plague, it seemed that every grasshopper had a worm in it, eventually spelling their demise. But for the ranchers and farmers, the damage was done. Hay and grain fields had been devastated, resulting in a lack of feed and income at a time when they could least afford it.

Winters

Despite the hot, dry summers that withered and burnt grass on the range and kept hay crops to a minimum, winters during the 1930s seemed to make up for the lack of summer moisture by dropping record snowfalls on the ranges. The winter of 1936 was a particularly bad one for the Cariboo. Harry Marriott, after detailing the casualties of an incredibly dry summer, commented that, "To climax the picture, we had an eight-inch fall of snow in the first ten days of November, and from then on we all knew what a rough, tough winter was like. The snow got real deep and we had at least six weeks of fifty-below-zero weather—and sometimes lower. The only time the thermometer improved was around the middle of the day when the temperature would generously rise to about twenty degrees above zero. As soon as the sun went down—down she'd drop again to forty-odd below."[6]

Marriot went on to tell of a trip he had made with a load of beef from his ranch to the railway stop at Kelly Lake. The distance was some 27 miles and the thermometer measured a bone-chilling 62 below. The snow lay deep and it was so cold that Marriott had to tie the reins to the wagon box and walk behind just to keep warm. Mile after mile, the team plodded along through waist-deep snow. When Marriott stopped the team to feed them some hay off the wagon, they were too cold to even eat. Marriott, extracting a frozen-solid sandwich from his pocket, felt the same way and returned the sandwich to its pocket. Finally, hours after dark at 9:30 that night, Marriott and his team arrived cold and exhausted at Kelly Lake. After a hot supper, a good sleep and a big breakfast, the team and their driver were back on the road home in the same conditions.

A couple of years later, Marriott had a hired man to winter-feed the cattle at a distant hay meadow. The man was staying in a cabin that had not been

Winter feeding on the Douglas Lake Ranch. John Bibby and his partner are dressed for warmth, not style. *Doug Cox photo*

used for years. The chinking had fallen out from between the logs in many places, allowing the frosty air to blow right through and the mice to enter at will. After contemplating the situation, Marriott arrived at a typical rancher's solution. When feeding the cattle, he would stand with an old shovel and wait until a cow lifted her tail. Then he would shovel up some of the hot fresh manure and run to the cabin to throw it into a crack in the logs. Within minutes, the manure would be frozen into place and before long the cabin was relatively air-tight and quite liveable.[7]

Fred Nichol, whose father, David, homesteaded in the Long Lake area south of Kamloops related coming back from town one particularly cold night with his father. The team was slowly working its way up the Corkscrew Hill with a load of lumber on the wagon when the horses shied off the road to avoid something in the way. Dave Nichol could see a man lying on the road and called out, "Who's that down there?" The fellow replied, "Move up a step, Dave, I think the wheel's on my neck." Then he returned to what was obviously a drunken stupor. The wagon's wheels were nowhere near the man, but his stiff collar, still the fashion in those days, made him think a wheel was resting on him. The Nichols loaded him up and took him home with them. He spent the rest of the winter with the family and worked for them.

The true test of a person's fortitude in the dead of winter was a visit to the outhouse, which was usually some distance from the house. One ranch had hired a young man named Charlie who had come from Birmingham, England, and was not familiar with outhouses, having had the luxury of indoor plumbing back home. He was also not used to the one-piece long wool underwear worn by all throughout the long British Columbia winters (and, for some, all summer as well). Charlie was introduced to both and became familiar with the long, cold walk to the outhouse as well as the "moment of contact" that could bring tears to even the toughest teamster's eyes. After some days, Charlie was asked how he liked the one-piece long johns. His reply, "It's real warm but I do hate to take off all my clothing when I go to the bathroom." Charlie had yet to discover the convenient "trap door" in the back of his underwear.[8]

Cattle Diseases

In the earliest days of ranching in British Columbia, infectious diseases were at a minimum. But as cattle were imported from other countries, particularly European ones, they started to appear more and more frequently. During the 1930s, several diseases became widespread enough to cause major losses to the ranchers, who were already reeling from dropping prices.

One of the first infectious diseases to appear on the ranches in the 1930s was hemorrhagic septicemia, commonly known as "cattle flu," which was most common among calves that were being weaned. The shock of removing a calf from its mother and the abrupt change from milk to forage made the calf more susceptible to the disease. Wet conditions and herding the calves too close together were also contributing factors. The first symptoms included a general dullness of the calf and a reluctance to move combined with a fever. This was followed by a swelling of the throat that quickly led to the poor animal suffocating. When the first symptoms appeared, a rancher had to act quickly, as the calf would usually collapse and die within 6 to 24 hours of the onset of the disease. Martha Furrer, who ranched with her husband, Victor, near Horse Lake in the Cariboo, told of an outbreak of hemorrhagic septicemia on their ranch in 1934. Some neighbours had brought in cattle from the Okanagan that were considered responsible for the disease. When the first symptoms appeared, Victor Furrer phoned the local veterinarian, who came out immediately and inoculated the calves. Despite his quick action, Furrer lost two head of cattle. However, most people in the area managed to inoculate in advance and, before long, all ranchers inoculated their calves at branding time to prevent the disease.[9]

Coccidiosis was a parasite that usually affected calves that were between one and six months old, but older cattle, especially one- and two-year-olds, could also be affected. Young calves were usually exposed to the parasite when they were turned out onto pasture that had been occupied by older infected cattle. The parasite has a 14-day incubation period so, by the time a rancher noticed the symptoms, there would be millions of germs in the calf's stomach. Typical signs of coccidiosis included diarrhea, a rough coat and a loss of appetite and weight. The advanced stage saw the calf pass strings of blood in its manure and sometimes take fits, throw itself down and grind its teeth. When the parasite first began to appear, ranchers would drench the calves with a beer bottle full of a mixture of sulphate of iron, sulphur and salol. This was only partially effective in stopping the spread. Before long ranchers learned that the Lederle Laboratories of Pearl River, New York, had developed a tablet of sulfaguanidine that effectively eliminated the parasite in three or four days. But the first major outbreak in British Columbia proved to be an expensive one, particularly on the larger ranches where an entire calf crop could be infected. The Gang Ranch alone lost over 400 calves from it in one season. Ranchers soon learned that it was easier to prevent the disease than to treat it. They began to watch closely for calves that were straining or had a dirty tail, and also examined their manure for signs of blood. As soon as any signs appeared, the infected calf and cow would be separated from the herd. Since the parasites thrived in a moist environment, keeping the calves on a particularly dry pasture and preventing overgrazing also helped. These practices were usually effective in controlling the spread of coccidiosis but the parasite continues to be a potential problem for cattle producers.

Another dreadful disease that took its toll on cattle in the 1930s was brucellosis, which also was parasitic in origin. Brucellosis was also called Bang's disease after the Danish veterinarian Bernard Bang who, in the 1890s, isolated the bacterium *Brucella abortus,* which is the principal cause of brucellosis in cattle. In cattle this disease was known as "contagious abortion" because it caused abortion or premature calving of infected animals, usually between the fifth and eighth month of pregnancy. Infected cows often suffered from a retained afterbirth, which made them sterile.

Rustling

As the Depression of the 1930s deepened and people became desperate for food and financial relief, the incidence of cattle rustling increased. There were two types of rustling. The more common practice was to steal unbranded calves, or to kill and butcher calves or unbranded yearlings on the spot for meat. A dressed, fat range calf, with the guts, hide, feet and head removed, would give 200 pounds of meat, an amount that could always be consumed quickly by a family and possibly their friends. Any greater quantity of meat, say from a large cow or steer, was more difficult to use up quickly and keep hidden from others. The rustler would pick a clear, moonlit night or early morning to do his dirty work. He would travel quietly through the bush and keep off the trails and roads where he might leave tracks or meet someone. He would try to get rid of the hide and offal by burying it or covering it with brush. The cow that had lost her calf would bawl for it in the area it was last seen, not too far from where it had been butchered, and would hang around for four or five days before giving up and going away. This type of rustling was most often an act of desperation by someone who was trying to feed his family and saw the nearby rancher as being able to afford to lose an animal here and there. Most ranchers felt that if the government allowed settlers to catch fish or to shoot deer, moose and small game out of season it would remove some of the temptation to rustle the rancher's stock.

Some rustlers devised more creative ways of getting their meat. One enterprising homesteader was known to ride out with a sack behind his saddle and steal a calf just a few days old. He would carry it back to his farm in the sack and put the calf on a gentle milk cow until it was big enough to butcher. This practice was dangerous because anyone passing by would question why a white-faced Hereford calf was on a milk cow. Other would-be thieves would just ride through the bush until they found a cow with a calf and shoot the cow in a secluded spot, leaving the body to rot. A day or so later, they would locate the calf and drive it back home and brand it. If a ranch was in an isolated area, the chance of getting away with this practice was much more likely as it could be weeks before a rancher located the remains of the cow.

Most settlers who were driven to butchering cattle to feed their families did not feel good about taking from their rancher neighbours who were, more often than not, in equally bad financial trouble. One former Douglas Lake Ranch employee felt so guilty after stealing and butchering a Douglas Lake steer that he shot himself in a cabin near Aspen Grove. The area has been known ever since as Suicide Valley.

The more serious type of rustling involved driving cattle into large trucks during the night and removing them by stealth before anyone knew they were gone. Although this was much less common—especially in British Columbia cattle country, where an unfamiliar truck carrying cattle was apt to arouse suspicion—it did happen. Most years, a few head disappeared and ranchers could find no trace of them. One year Victor Furrer, who ranched in a remote area near Horse Lake in the Cariboo, lost 22 head and another year 11 head. His neighbours, the Larsons, tried to prevent cattle rustling by moving their cattle way back into the bush but they still lost some. When someone blamed the losses on bears, Larson said, "Bears don't carry knives."

Butch Helwig, who had come all the way from California to the remote Nazko Valley, must have thought he was far enough away from civilization to be sure he wouldn't have to deal with rustlers. But in the late summer of 1932, when he went to round up his cattle that had been turned out on the range in the spring, he found that 100 head of cows and calves were missing. Someone had watched very closely so that they knew Helwig would turn out his cattle and leave them for a couple of months before roundup. By the time he discovered that the cattle were missing, the trail was stone cold. Nonetheless, he hired Johnny Sam, the best Native tracker in the area, to try and find the trail. They searched for the cattle for three months but could not find them. They did, however, find two or three of the holding places where the cattle had been kept, which gave them an idea of the direction that the cattle had gone in. But eventually the cattle were driven through range with other cattle grazing on it and tracking them became useless. By fall, many of the cows had wandered back to the herd but the unbranded calves had been mixed into someone else's herd. Helwig, who had slowly built up his herd through hard work and sacrifice, lost two-thirds of his calf crop and several cows, not to mention the time and wages spent tracking them. Despite this setback he continued to ranch in the Nazko Valley.[10]

Cowgirls

Ranching on the small ranches in the Interior of British Columbia was hard work, and before children started school they were expected to contribute, regardless of their gender. This was not so much a matter of gender equality as downright necessity. On isolated ranches every available hand was required to make ends meet. Daughters and sons worked side by side during roundup and branding, and performed myriad chores to help their parents. Some daughters thrived in the freedom of working in the outdoors and developed a particular affinity for the ranching way of life. They spent much of their adult lives riding and roping alongside the cowboys, who in most cases were happy to have the help and quite accepting of women working with them. The cowgirls were inevitably superb horsewomen and wise in the ways of cattle and horses. They played a significant role in the development of ranching in the province and quietly contributed to the way of life of the rancher.

Paddy Cripps

Frances Patricia (Paddy) Cripps was born in 1907, the daughter of Alkali Lake Ranch owners Charles and Mary Wynn Johnson. She grew up at Alkali Lake, and spent as much time as possible astride a horse. As a young girl, she went to see the first Williams Lake Stampede, where Leonard Palmantier, who was breaking horses at the Alkali Lake ranch, was riding in the rodeo. She was captivated by the strength and finesse that Palmantier displayed and became determined to develop her own abilities as a cowgirl, which she did through countless hours of practice. Her skill at riding and roping made her indispensable at branding time on the ranch in early July. Paddy helped to round up 700 or 800 cows and calves, and then roped the calves and dragged them to the branding fire. In 1929 she married Pack Harris and they had two children, Jim and Cherie. The couple purchased the Big Lake Ranch and, after Pack passed away, Paddy ran the ranch and worked part-time at the local stockyards. She was a dedicated rancher and an active community member. In 1941 Paddy married Harold Cripps and the couple had three children, Julie, Wade and Clint. They sold the Big Lake Ranch in 1956 and purchased Chilako Ranch near Prince George, operating it until 1970. Paddy was a working cowgirl until her death in 1983.

Cowgirls racing at a local rodeo in the Okanagan. All of these women are riding western saddles, the sidesaddle having become a thing of the past for serious cowgirls. *Historic O'Keefe Ranch photo*

Mary Ann Ross

Mary Ann Ross was born in the Kleena Kleene Valley on April 1, 1913. She was the daughter of George Turner, an American relocated to the Chilcotin, and Louisa One Eye, daughter of Chilcotin Chief One Eye. Her parents raised both horses and cattle at Kleena Kleene and Mary Ann learned ranching from them. She was an excellent equestrian and began working with cattle when she was

about six years old. Mary Ann married Jim Ross, who ranched near Redstone with his brothers. After their marriage, the couple worked at the Gang Ranch and later for the C1 Ranch before buying a place at Charlotte Lake. Mary Ann worked alongside the men in all aspects of ranch life, whether it was putting up hay, feeding cattle, rounding up or riding the range. She could spend long hours in the saddle without seeming to tire and gained a reputation as a top hand, an excellent craftsperson and a good cook. Jim and Mary Ann had 12 children. Mary Ann passed away in Williams Lake in July 2001.

Alex and Ann Paxton, Peavine Springs Ranch. Ann was an excellent cowgirl, packer and guide. *Museum of the Cariboo Chilcotin, Williams Lake photo*

Ann Paxton

Ann Paxton was the daughter of Hortense and Frank English, born in 1913 at Four Mile Creek. Ann was a hard-working, capable cowgirl who competed for many years in the Williams Lake Stampede riding racehorses. In 1933, she won the Silver Cup in the Pony Express race. In the mid-1940s, Ann married Alex Paxton, who was a cowboy at the Chilco Ranch. The couple bought Spain Lake Ranch, six miles west of Alexis Lake in the Chilcotin, in 1949 and ran a guiding business at Spain Lake. Ann was also an excellent packer and guide. When the Pelaire Mine was opened on the windswept mountain above Falls Creek near Taskeko Lake in the south Chilcotin, Ann and Alex packed heavy awkward loads of mining equipment and supplies up the steep mountain to the mine site at 12,792 feet, the highest mine in North American at the time. Ann cooked for the crew halfway up the mountain while the top of the peak was being prepared as a mining camp. She and Alex competed together and won team roping events for many years. They stayed at Spain Lake Ranch until 1970, when they sold to Amady Isnardy and bought property in Alexis Creek where they lived until Ann's death in 1986. Alex survived her until 1999.

Dolly Barber

Dolly Barber (née Marsel) was born in 1918 near Olalla, between Penticton and Keremeos, the daughter of Joe Marsel and Julia Surprise (corrupted from Suprenant). She was the youngest of 11 children and got her basic schooling in Olalla before starting work on the Marsel Ranch owned by her father. Although the ranch raised sheep, pigs, chickens and turkeys, its main focus was Hereford cattle and horses. The horses grazed on the mountains west of the road and Dolly used to spend hours chasing horses, an activity that she remembered with glee:

> Have you ever been on a wild horse chase? Well, if not, you've missed out! You go down the hill, and you can't see anything for dust really. One time one of my nephews was coming behind me and he said, "You know with the mane of your horse flying, and your long hair flying and blending with the horse's tail, it looks like one being!" Oh yes, when you come out of there all of you that can be seen is eyes because of the dust! It was fun, but it's kind of dangerous. My mom used to have a fit every time this happened. She'd say, "You go out there and you're just wild!"[11]

Dolly would help round up, brand and castrate the horses, and then help with the breaking. She married Reginald (Reg) Barber in 1944 and he immediately went off to war. Dolly stayed on the family ranch, put up hay and fed cattle through the winter. After the war, she and Reg took over the operation of the ranch and operated it successfully until the 1960s. At time of writing, Dolly, now in her 90s, still lives in her home in Olalla near Keremeos.

June Charlton

June Charlton was born in Walhachin, BC, on September 6, 1919, to Bud and Dora Walters, the youngest of six children. Bud, who owned a ranch on Deadman Creek, was a noted bronc rider and taught all his children, including June, the finer points of riding. On one occasion, he watched her get bucked off and told her, "Get back on and don't dare grab the saddle horn this time. If you hadn't grabbed it you wouldn't have fell off." She quickly re-mounted and rode the horse to a standstill. At the age of eight she was helping with haying by driving a hay sloop pulled by a big Clyde mare. June and her sister Rita were the first two women in BC to hold a big-game guide licence. She rode with Herb Matier chasing wild horses on Tobacco Mountain. When Bud sold his cattle, June bought some of her own and registered her own brand. In

1946, she married Bill Charlton and the couple raised two boys. At the age of 50, she joined a riding club and started to get involved in gymkhana so that she could show the young girls how a real cowgirl could ride!

Horses and Other Beasts of Burden

At the beginning of the 1930s, it looked like the tractor would soon take over from the workhorse on the ranches and farms of the Interior. But, as the Depression progressed, the price of gasoline made tractors less than economical. Once again, the noble horse was in demand, selling for anywhere from $40 to $100 a head, while cattle were commanding $4 to $20 each. Horse ranchers, who for years had watched their market dwindle as the tractor took over more and more ranch work, suddenly found themselves with a valuable commodity. Workhorses were in demand again.

Many ranches turned their horses loose to fend for themselves on the upland ranges, frequently government-leased land. These vast areas were only sparsely fenced and the horses were quite wild, having spent most of their early life far from the taming influence of man. Each band of horses was under the control of a stallion, which protected and defended his harem against all intruders, including other stallions. Mares, even though they had no conception of belonging to anyone, were branded and turned loose to propagate. Their colts were left with their moms for the first four years of their lives. Compared to animals in the ranches where mares and colts were kept confined in pastures, these horses were fearful of humans and quite wild when contained in a small space.

Every spring, the horse ranchers rounded up the various bands of horses and ran them into the home corrals. As each separate band came together, the stallions would attempt to keep their harems away from the other bunches, making it extremely difficult to contain the combined bands. When the herd came together, the stallions would immediately confront each other, rearing up and striking with their front feet. The veteran stallions were battle-scarred from many a previous encounter where their opponent's teeth or feet had scored. When the entire herd was driven into a holding area, the battle between the stallions reached a frenzy point and they frequently had to be separated and held in small pens. Once in the holding area, the young studs were separated out to be broken and sold. But, before the training could begin, each of the frisky young horses had to be castrated and branded. Since this experience was hard on a horse, the studs were put into a pasture where they could feed on the spring grass and fatten up. By May, they were sleek and fat and in much better condition to withstand the trauma of castration.

At the Willow Ranch, operated by the Bulman family, about 60 or 70 head of two- to four-year-olds were handled each spring. Roping the young studs, especially the strapping four-year-olds, was a challenge. It took a crew of five or six cowboys a full two days to catch them one by one for the operation. Unlike cattle, which are most often roped by the back feet, horses have to be forefooted, which involves roping the front feet. Once the front feet were secure, three or four cowboys wearing stout leather gloves would grab the rope and hang on for dear life, eventually throwing the horse on the ground and tying it down. Then, as quickly as possible, one cowboy would run to the fire for a branding iron while another cowboy deftly performed the operation. The gelding was then turned loose in a corral to await breaking.[12]

The market in the 1930s was primarily for workhorses and the method of breaking for harness was quite different from breaking saddle horses. First of all, the unbroken horses would be driven into a chute where they could be fitted with a halter. A strong manilla hemp rope would be tied around their necks with a bowline knot and looped through the ring at the bottom of the halter. Once the horses were out of the chute, this rope would be secured to a ring on the stout snubbing post in the centre of the corral. This ring was attached to an iron band that was in a groove so that it could rotate around the post. As in breaking a horse for saddle, each animal had to be "sacked out" to accustom it to being touched in all areas. The gunny sack was attached to a long pole so that the horse could be sacked out at a distance.

Douglas Lake Clydesdales, Chapperon Lake, 1930. These gentle giants did all of the heavy pulling on the ranch. *Doug Cox photo*

Once the horses had settled down a bit and were considered halter-broken, they were fitted with a bridle and their heads tied around tight to one side for half an hour, and then the other side for the same amount of time. This made them "bridle wise" as they would have to learn to respond to the reins steering them when they were in harness. Then they were turned over to the "skinner" who would be responsible for training them to pull various instruments.

The secret to breaking a horse for team work was to harness it for the first while with a calm, experienced workhorse. Outfits like the Willow Ranch had several older "breaking horses" that would be hitched with a colt for its first few drives. These "bomb-proof" horses knew exactly what was happening and had a calming influence on the colts. For the first drive, the skinner would use a heavy wagon with strong, wide wheels and the neck yoke would be tied solidly to the pole in the middle. This was to ensure that, if the traces became unhooked during a runaway, the wagon tongue would remain attached and manageable. The wagon would be rolled alongside a barn wall, where the colt was tied by the halter while the team was hitched to the wagon. This prevented the colt from making a premature run before all the rigging was in place. Then, when everything was in proper order, the skinner would call to a cowboy at the colt's head, "Turn him loose!" and the fun would begin.

Most young horses, full of nervous energy, would spring forward and run like deer. The skinner would run them in a circle with the old, experienced horse on the inside. This would make it easier to pull the breaking horse around and the young colt, with its head tied to the collar of the older horse had little choice but to follow. After several trips around the yard at breakneck speed, the colt would begin to calm down and the skinner would head the team out toward a large field. The young horse, seeing its beloved hills in the distance, would once again set off at a dead run, kicking and bucking and often getting tangled up in the harness.

This hell-bent-for-leather ride was exciting and dangerous. But Dolly Barber, who grew up at the Marsel Ranch near Olalla in the Similkameen, loved to get on board. "I used to like to get on the wagon when they were breaking horses, because you were going to have a run and the field was rough! My brother didn't want me on there either, but I'd get on at the last minute and he'd have his hands full with the horses, so he could get rid of me! I don't know why, I was just with horses from day one."[13]

All this excitement was sure to draw a crowd if there was anyone around. This was certainly the case at the Bulman's Circle J Ranch near Westwold, where the workhorses were broken across the road from the Westwold schoolhouse. One of the students, Bill Portman, who was attending the school in 1932, remembered:

> The outstanding disturbance that up-set [*sic*] classes was the "horse breaking" activity originating from the Bulman ranch. To train a horse for farm use, a wild horse was hitched up with a trained work-horse with various paraphernalia to hook them together. In addition, two men sat atop a large wagon with high sides and a breaking system. One man drove the team, the other manned the break. It seemed this wagon would go thundering by on the gravel road adjacent to the schoolhouse every day when we were in class. Teachers gave up on controlling the rush of spectators to see this boisterous, bucking, hollering road show go careening wildly down the highway. It took about half-an-hour for the dust (and us) to settle back to normal.[14]

After three or four drives, the colt would begin to understand the drill and settle down to work in harness. The Bulmans and others broke horses to harness in rapid succession and shipped carloads by train to Chilliwack and Edmonton, where they were purchased as workhorses for farms in these areas.

Mules were also broken for harness but they proved to be quite a different sort of animal. The Bulmans had a huge, ugly Spanish mammoth jack donkey that they used to breed mares to produce mules that they trained for harness as well. The debate between horse people and mule people about the usefulness of their chosen animal began with the first mule and continues today. There is no question that each breed brings its own advantages and disadvantages to farm work. "Mules have a high tolerance for heat, need less water, as a rule are easier keepers, are capable of long periods of hard work, have a phenomenal memory, hold a grudge for a long time, live to get even, are difficult to train, and know that they are beautiful," said Lynn Miller. "Horses have a high tolerance for work, are usually trustworthy, are extremely sensitive, can be as dumb as their owners, seldom hold a grudge, want to please, are easy to train, will eat to excess, seldom forget a nightmare, and don't have a clue how beautiful they are."[15]

The Bulmans found that mules were quite different in their reactions to certain situations. If they roped a horse around the neck and snubbed it to a post, it would fight and never let the rope go slack until it choked and fell over. A roped mule, on the other hand, would fight for a few minutes and take a couple of hard runs to the end of the rope and then stand still and sulk. "They were smarter than horses and learned very quickly," said Alex Bulman.

"If they had any notions of kicking though we had to watch out for, unlike horses, they didn't just kick to cause a commotion. They would usually wait until a target was within range when their little black hard hoofs would fly back like trip hammers. We had a lot of respect for those hind feet."[16]

One time, Bulman and his crew were driving about 150 horses, including two stallions, into corrals along with the jack donkey. The stallions took the opportunity to gang up on the donkey. During the battle, some of the horses and the jack donkey were forced into a fence and became entangled in barbed wire. The horses, when they felt tangled up in the wire, went crazy, kicking and squirming, and were cut up quite badly. The jack donkey instead of panicking, settled down on the ground and, when the turmoil stopped, carefully stepped out of the wire and walked away.

Another jack donkey achieved notoriety throughout ranching country. Jimmy Murdock, an old-time horseman, owned a donkey that he named Abraham. When he grew tired of Abraham, Murdock sold raffle tickets on him. Ralph Overton's wife traded Murdock a dozen eggs for a raffle ticket and won Abraham! Ralph had the grand idea of incorporating Abraham into his rodeo clown act; fortunately, the donkey proved to be a great performer and easily trained. Ralph trained him with apples and candy to lift his leg, lie down and count. He would also lie down on top of Ralph, much to the delight of the audience. One time at the Kamloops Rodeo a Native boy was bothering Ralph so he had Abraham lie down on the boy. Ralph removed one boot at a time and threw them to the audience and pretended to be unable to get Abraham to move while the audience roared with delight. Another time, after a long winter's gap between performances, Ralph got the donkey to lie down on him but unfortunately Abraham had forgotten his training. Ralph pounded the ground for some time before anyone realized that he really was trapped under the donkey.

Abraham retired on the Overton ranch at Fairview and was allowed to run on the range with the mares. The little donkey was not considered large enough to breed the mares but, in a classic version of "Where there's a will, there's a way," Abraham would bite and chase the mares until he got them onto a hillside. Using the slope of the hill for added height, he was quite successful in breeding the mares. He was so successful, in fact, that all Overton's mares had little mules the next spring. Overton, not being overly fond of mules, decided to have Abraham castrated. He asked Abraham's old trainer Ralph to drop by for the operation and he instructed Abraham, "Come on, Abe, lay down." Obedient to a fault, Abraham lay down. The operation complete, Abraham got up and placidly began to eat grass, apparently not wanting to give Ralph the satisfaction of seeing him in pain. Abraham lived happily into old age on the Overton ranch.[17]

In the fall of 1936 there was a horse roundup in the south Okanagan for a different purpose. The Communist government in Russia needed food for its starving people and sent refrigerator boats to Vancouver for horse meat. There were two different roundups in Canada, one on the Prairies and one in the Okanagan. The Okanagan roundup was coordinated by Will Haynes and herds were driven from different locations to the Kettle Valley Railway in Penticton. One large herd of wild horses was gathered from the hills and corralled at the Brent ranch on Shingle Creek west of Penticton. The drive started at 2:30 in the morning and about 200 head of horses left the holding area on the run, kicking up huge clouds of dust. Once they settled down, they slowed to a jog and by the time they arrived in Penticton they were walking. Another big herd had been gathered at Val Haynes' place by Osoyoos and Okanagan Native Eneas Sussap brought in 600 horses.

Once in Penticton, the crew of Russians took over. There were several veterinarians and other crew members, all sporting long beards as if they had just stepped out from the pages of a picture book! The horses were run through a chute and then covered with a net made of heavy rope so they couldn't move. The vets would check the horse for blemishes and, if it was acceptable, brand the left forefoot. Although the Russians bought a lot of horses, they were very selective and rejected the old, sick and blemished. The acceptable horses were purchased for a 1¼ cents a pound and averaged $18.50 a head. There were also several carloads of horses driven off the Bald Range into Faulder on the Kettle Valley Railway and shipped from there, most probably to Vladivostok. The roundup was a humanitarian effort to feed the starving Russians.

Trail Dust and Mountain Passes

For ranchers in the remote areas of the Interior, the only way to move cattle, either to distant ranges or to market, was by driving them. Long cattle drives had not changed in the 70 years since the gold rush days of the 1860s. Good men and good horses were still the essential requirements for moving cattle and the long, narrow cattle trails were still the only routes.

The Western Canadian Ranching Company, whose British interests were headed by London publisher Thomas Galpin, who had purchased the Gang Ranch from Thaddeus Harper in 1891, still owned the ranch in the 1930s. As well as the huge 160,000 acres of the main ranch, it had various other smaller holdings, including the Perry Ranch and Lot 44 north of the Chilcotin River, which, at 8,900 acres, was said to be the largest "lot" in the province. In addition to its deeded land, the Gang Ranch had huge government leases adjoining its various properties. One of these leases, called the Ply-U, was located at the headwaters of Deadman Creek, some distance from the main Perry Ranch property. In June 1932, the Gang Ranch hired range rider Cliff Brousseau to move a herd of 350 steers from the Perry Ranch to the Ply-U. Cliff, in turn, hired Jack Walters and Johnny Burke, the latter a Native cowboy from the Deadman Reserve. They were joined by two Alberta cowboys on their way to the Cariboo, Jock Bannerman and Ed Sheed. Jimmy Wilson, grandson of Johnny Wilson, the BC Cattle King, was hired on as chuckwagon cook.

The first challenge was to round up the cattle from a vast area on the Perry Ranch. The men worked in teams of two, bringing the steers to a corner pasture and holding them against the fence. During the day, as the teams spread out to gather more steers, Jock would allow them to spread out a little for feed and water before bunching them in the corner for the night. The men were fortunate enough to be able to sleep in an unfinished two-storey cabin with no doors or windows. The BC cowboys took great delight in telling the somewhat naive Alberta boys about the plentiful rattlesnakes in the area but succeeded in scaring themselves in the process. The entire crew slept upstairs in the cabin and, just to be safe, knocked out the bottom three stairs to prevent rattlesnakes from visiting them during the night.

When the steers were finally all gathered, the cowboys started to drive them to the Ply-U, about 50 miles away. They kept a leisurely pace of about 10 miles a day so the steers could graze along the way. Jimmy Wilson would drive the team and chuckwagon to a spot where the steers could be kept for the night and set up camp. By the time the cowboys arrived and the steers were settled down, Jimmy had prepared a supper of boiled potatoes and vegetables, canned milk and corned beef. The crew slept under trees and removed only their hats and boots to sleep. The BC cowboys had bedrolls consisting of two saddle blankets and the Alberta boys had the luxury of sleeping bags. The crew wrangled the horses at three in the morning and, after a hearty breakfast of pancakes, bacon and eggs washed down with coffee, were in the saddle by five. Often it was nine in the evening before the men were back at the chuckwagon, taking just enough time to eat and climb into their bedrolls. All this for the grand wage of $1 a day.

One morning Jimmy had the chuckwagon parked on a little hill and was serving breakfast. One of the saddle horses that were tied to different parts of the wagon got spooked by something. He began to pull back on his halter shank and that got the other horses spooked so that they also began to pull at their reins. The pulling started the chuckwagon rolling down the hill, which spooked the horses even worse, breaking halters and bridle reins. The wagon gathered speed as it travelled downhill about 150 yards before it came to a stop, none the worse for wear. The cattle drive started late that morning as the cowboys mended halters, bridles and reins and Jimmy had to wrangle his team to pull the chuckwagon back to the road.

After returning to the Perry Ranch for their pay, the cowboys split up to go their separate ways. Jock and Ed headed to the Cariboo but weren't there for long, finding that the Depression had dried up the work. They ended up working for Jack Walters' dad, Budd, on the haying crew. Some years later, Jock Bannerman was working as a range rider for the Cornwalls at Cherry Creek when he accidently shot himself. He died alone in a cabin on an isolated range.[18]

In the Anahim Lake area, getting cattle to market was a community activity. Every rancher in the area was involved in the roundup and those who wanted to sell their cattle at the stockyards in Williams Lake, some 330 miles away, put their cattle in one herd to be driven to market. In the fall of 1938, Ed Collett and Russell Overton were hired to drive the herd to market but, for the first day, the whole community came with them to get the cattle settled in to the trail. Lester Dorsey, who had a large number of cattle in the herd, stayed on for another two days until he was sure that the herd would not decide to turn around and go home. On the narrow trail from Anahim

George Powers driving cattle on the Chilcotin trail. The drive from Anahim Lake through the Chilcotin to Williams Lake covered 330 miles. *Museum of the Cariboo Chilcotin, Williams Lake photo*

Lake, a wagon was out of the question, so the two cowboys packed all their food and necessities on pack horses. For the first leg of their drive, they had been given a huge piece of moose meat that they hung up at night to keep cool and wrapped up and put on the pack horse during the day. They fried up a couple of moose-meat steaks every day until the meat was gone. After that they subsisted on rice with canned salmon mixed in.

Their route from Anahim was right over the mountains to Chezacut and then south until they struck the Williams Lake road. From then on there were holding pastures along the way where the cattle could be held for the night. When they reached the Fraser River they were joined by the Ross brothers of Chezacut, who added another hundred or so head of cattle. The two herds were held together on the west side of the old wooden Chimney Creek bridge and were brought across 10 head at a time as that was all the bridge would hold at one time. That meant 25 trips over the bridge to get all the combined herds across. When that time-consuming process was complete, the cattle had to be hurried into Williams Lake to be loaded onto the Pacific Great Eastern train to Squamish. There was not enough time to separate the two different herds and so they were all quickly loaded into cattle cars as the train was ready to leave. Ed and Russell rode in the coach to Squamish, which at that time was the end of the line. The cattle cars were then loaded onto a barge to Vancouver where they were shunted onto tracks

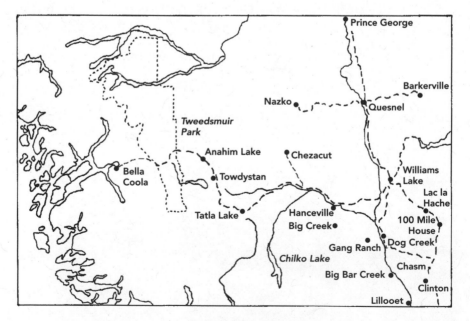

The Cariboo-Chilcotin

and taken to the stockyards. Ed was the only one who could identify the different brands and had to sort the cattle out so that their respective owners could be paid. In those days, a prime steer was worth about $20. Once the sorting was complete, the cowboys had to go by train back to Williams Lake and then to Anahim Lake on horseback.[19]

With cattle selling for $20 per head, the market had not improved and it remained low throughout the 1930s. This prompted Arthur Knoll of Chezacut to try driving his cattle in the opposite direction from the Anahim drive. He hoped that he would get a better price in Vancouver than in Williams Lake and decided to drive his cattle over the mountains to Bella Coola and then travel by boat to Vancouver. He was not sure the route was feasible so he contracted Alfred Bryant, who was a big-game guide in the area, to take him and his son, Ollie, over the route to see if it was possible. They decided it was, and in September 1939 Ollie set out west from Chezacut with 200 head of two-year-old steers and a few dry cows. Top cowboys were required for this drive and Ollie's list included some of the finest cowboys in the Chilcotin at the time: Alfred Bryant, Thomas Squinas, Bert Matthews and Wes Jasper Jr., and Gordon McTaggart as cook. They pushed their cattle west on the trail through the mountains and reached Towdystan, south of Anahim Lake, two days later. They camped at Aktaklin Lake and then drove the cattle along the Dean River through Anahim Lake and northward to Capoose Crossing where they crossed the Dean and headed west into Tweedsmuir Park. The crew made camp wherever there was some pasture for the cattle and slept without shelter in bedrolls on the ground despite the high altitudes and cold fall weather. Two men had to ride night herd throughout the trip to keep the cattle from wandering off and to watch for any predators that might be hungry for beef. For five days, the cowboys struggled along the old trail through the Coast Mountains. Feed was scarce and the cowboys were weary and sore when they finally reached the downhill side of the mountains. It proved to be the toughest stretch of all, as it dropped 6,000 feet straight down and took an entire day to navigate. The cowboys each drove 20 head of cattle in front of them, along the steep, narrow trail with a sheer drop on one side. But all 200 head reached Bella Coola safely and were loaded onto a scow for the trip down the coast. Ollie Knoll and Wes Jasper Jr. accompanied the cattle on their 30-hour voyage to Vancouver, where they met Arthur and Anna Knoll, who had driven down by car to watch the sale and then drive Ollie and Wes home. Ironically, the sale was a complete disappointment, with the cattle bringing in two cents a pound less than they were selling for in Williams Lake the same day. The beef drive to Williams Lake would have taken 13 days whereas the long trek to Vancouver took 17 days. In later years, Ollie summed it up, "A long, hard drive and no money in it. We never marketed our beef that way again." But they did make history.

Cattle Buyers versus Ranchers

In the 1930s, there were no fewer than six packing plants operating in Vancouver: Burns, Swifts, Canada Packers, Pacific Meats, Gainers and Alberta Meats. As the packing industry developed to serve BC's growing population, a stockyard was constructed in Vancouver to serve as a marketing centre for the entire province. Most of the ranchers felt, and with good reason, that the packers were in cahoots with each other to fix prices and to divvy up the cattle market so there was not too much competition or, at best, just the illusion of competition. It was no secret that the leading packers in Vancouver held weekly meetings and the cattlemen believed that at these get-togethers they would agree on what the top price of cattle would be in the week to come.

To make matters worse, ranchers were by nature an independent lot and there was no exchange of market information or unity among cattlemen. As Alex Bulman put it, "We were being picked off one at a time, there was no exchange of market information and we were desperate to get better prices for our cattle." [20]

Williams Lake stockyards, 1939. By the end of the 1930s, ranchers had realized they had to work together to market their cattle. *Museum of the Cariboo Chilcotin, Williams Lake photo*

Harry Marriott pointed out that "the widespread difference in prices the producer is paid, in comparison to the prices the consumer has to pay, is always a bitter reflection in the mind of the ranchers. I remember receiving four cents a pound for good steers by live weight, and the following day in a big department store in Vancouver, I paid twenty-two cents a pound for a humble pot roast, or chuck roast as it is called, which is just one jump ahead of boiling beef and stew bones."[21]

The ranchers' pent-up frustration and anger was focused on the cattle buyers. Each of the big meat packers had buyers in the field who were joined by independent buyers who purchased cattle province-wide and shipped them to the Vancouver stockyard for resale or to be sent directly to the meat packers. As might be expected, these buyers were not out to help ranchers make the most for their cattle but to make the most for their respective companies or, in the case of independent buyers, for themselves. Most of the buyers took full advantage of the ranchers, knowing that they had to sell their cattle to survive. They were a perishable product and could only be held for so long. Harry Marriott put it succinctly: "The real rugged deals handed out to some of the small ranchers was [sic] lower down than a snake's ass in a wagon track, but was quite legal. On one of my brand inspection trips to the stockyards on the PGE I heard a beef buyer blowing real hard, and telling how his company

had given him a thousand dollar Christmas present for doing such a real good job of chiselling on prices to the ranchers, so I figured it sure must have paid real good for them. The buyers had all the cattlemen over a barrel anyway."[22]

Harry Durrell, who owned the Wineglass Ranch near Riske Creek, expressed the attitude of most of the ranchers:

> At shipping time, there'd be buyers from several firms like Burns, Swifts, Canada Packers and that was about it. Oh, we really got bogged, you know. If there was only one there, and there often was, you just took what he offered. Even when there were two or three there, I'm sure there was a lot of collusion . . . I'm quite certain that, before they started, one would say, "I'll make a low offer on the cows and leave them to you but I want the steers." I'm sure they did. There was a lot of bitterness on the part of the ranchers.

Durrell went on to tell the story of Chauncy Maxwell, who earned the applause of many ranchers who were frustrated with the cattle buyers' offers. Maxwell had pre-empted a meadow 20 miles north of Chezacut, far off the beaten track and had driven his cattle to Williams Lake.

> A man named Maxwell from Chezacut sold his cattle to a Swift buyer who was very unpopular. His price might have been as good as other people but he was kind of offensive mannered. He bought Maxwell's cattle and Maxwell didn't like his manner. Maxwell was kind of an amateur boxer and fighter so Maxwell got gassed up a bit and got to thinking about it and met the cattle buyer in the Lakeview Hotel and floored him. Crawford, the buyer, he didn't like it too much so he gave Roland Tressiera $10 or $20 to clean up on Maxwell. So Tressiera tackled Maxwell and Maxwell flattened him right out like that too. So the buyer got flattened and wasted $20.[23]

Maxwell's encounter with Crawford was the talk of the ranching community for some time and, as Jack Durrell put it, "warmed a lot of ranchers' hearts."

Another incident illustrates the frustration that ranchers were feeling when their cattle were barely bringing in enough to cover the cost of raising them. John McCuddy had established a ranch and stopping house near Camp McKinney in the South Okanagan. After the mine at Camp McKinney ceased operations, McCuddy had to drive his cattle over the mountains to Greenwood in the Boundary area, where there was still some mining activity. McCuddy would ride ahead and ensure that there was a market for his cattle before driving them such a distance. On one occasion, he met with the cattle buyer at Greenwood and negotiated a fair price for his cattle and then returned home, rounded up the cattle and started them on the trail. After a few days, the cattle had reached Midway, about 10 miles from Greenwood, and McCuddy went on to let the cattle buyer know that the cattle were coming. The buyer figured that, since McCuddy was already committed, he had him at a disadvantage and offered him a much lower price. McCuddy made no response to the buyer but headed back to Midway where he rented the Naden Ranch and purchased a barn full of hay. Then he hired a butcher and slaughtered a few head of cattle a week, took them to Greenwood and sold the beef to stores and hotels in Greenwood and Phoenix all through the winter. Before long, the cattle buyer was visiting McCuddy and offering him a much better price. But McCuddy refused his offer as he was making much better money selling the beef on his own. Once again, the situation was the source of some much-needed amusement for the cattlemen in the area.

As the 1930s drew to a close and cattle prices began to rise again, ranchers continued to talk about getting together for the purposes of marketing their cattle. Within a few years, things would slowly change the lot of the ranchers as they banded together to form marketing organizations. But, for most, the 1930s had been a time of great hardship and challenge. Many had found it too much to handle and had sold out and moved on.

Everything from a Needle to a Wagon

The old-time general store was a rich mix of sights and smells that would overwhelm first-time customers. Bolts of bright cotton prints and bins of household supplies packed the walls; lanterns and harnesses hung from the ceiling; glass display cases highlighted jewellery and luxuries that most visitors could only look at longingly; the rich smells of kerosene, coffee and spices permeated the air and, to the children at least, the row of stick candy was immediately eye-catching. Long before the modern department store came into being, the general store provided everything that the isolated ranchers and their wives could need. And anything that was not available could be ordered and would be there within a week. The store was the heart of every ranching community, the home of the post office and repository for the community news. In the winter, the pot-bellied stove provided more than just heat to the visitor; it was the gathering place for those whose lives were made richer by their visit. In the 1930s, when incomes were reduced to a trickle and the rancher's payday came but once a year, the general stores functioned as banks, extending credit until better times came.

The 153 Mile Ranch at the time the Crosinas settled there. The Crosinas operated the general store from 1912 to the 1960s. *Museum of the Cariboo Chilcotin, Williams Lake photo*

In the south Cariboo, Robertson Brothers' Store in Clinton served this need. James and Raymond Robertson operated the store and their generous extension of credit to any resident of the vast area they served saved many a rancher struggling to feed his family. Harry Marriott remarked, "In all my years in South Cariboo I have never known of one instance where a real worthwhile, hard-working settler was refused credit in the line of buying a sack of flour and necessary grub."[24] The good grace of the Robertsons was seldom betrayed. Ranchers considered the credit they received as a sacred trust and made every effort to repay their benefactors.

Hilary Place, who operated the Ranchers Retail store at Dog Creek during the 1940s, often mentions leaving a store full of customers waiting for the mail to arrive while he went home for lunch, knowing that he could trust them. On only one occasion was he surprised to learn that one of his customers, who had served in the Second World War, had taken a flashlight without paying for it. When the man returned to the store, Place gently reminded him, "Johnnie . . . if you needed a flashlight and didn't have the money to buy one, why didn't you tell me and I'd give you one . . . You have earned your good name both here at home and during the war. I consider you a good friend and if you ever need something, come and see me and I'll do my best to get it for you." With tears in his eyes, Johnnie confessed his mistake, the two men shook hands, and the incident was forgotten.[25]

The same situation prevailed at Crosina's 153 Mile stopping house and store. Louis Crosina left his native Italy at the age of 15 and after working at various jobs in the Cariboo married Clara Noble, the school teacher at Lac la Hache. Clara had vowed that she would never run a roadhouse but, when the couple took up a pre-emption at 153 Mile in 1903, it was only a matter of time. The Native people who worked on the Crosina ranch were never interested in being paid in money, preferring "just a little bit of grub" instead, so Clara purchased a set of scales to weigh out produce in lieu of wages. Soon people in the neighbourhood would drop by and ask to purchase produce or other goods and the store was on its way. Before long, the Crosinas had built a two-storey log home that, to make ends meet, was opened to travellers on the Cariboo Road. For a time, the store was located in the stopping house but, in 1912, they constructed a general store across the road from the stopping house. The store became an institution in the area. Clara served all-comers with the same genial hospitality that she showed in the stopping house. She was always a friend of the Native people who frequented the store and sold their birch-bark baskets, tanned leather jackets and beadwork.

Louis Crosina was also a talented blacksmith. One of his four children, Lillian (known as Lily), suffered from rickets as a small child, which can lead to a softening of the bones and cause permanently bowed legs. To avoid this, Louis forged little metal braces to support Lily's legs as they grew. As Lily continued to grow, Louis forged larger braces until, as a teenager, Lily could discard them permanently and walk with straight, strong legs. Lil, as she became known to everyone, took particular pleasure in helping with the store and, when her mother died in 1936, she took over its operation. Her father moved away soon after and Lily bought the store and stopping house from him. She closed the stopping house in 1939 because of the shortage of labour at the outset of the Second World War. She carried on running the ranch with the help of Bryson Patenaude but focused on her first love, the store. She was known throughout the area for her friendly service. Customers from distant Horsefly and Beaver Valley would phone in their orders and Lil would package them up and send them out on the stage. She spoke the Secwepemc (Shuswap) language fluently and was loved by the people of the nearby Sugarcane Reserve. Lil suffered a heart attack in 1957 and took a year off to recuperate; she was behind the counter of her beloved store when she suffered another heart attack and died in 1963.

A similar story of commitment and community is found in the Lee's grocery store at Hanceville in the Chilcotin. Norman Lee had opened a trading post in the 1890s and, after he married Agnes Lee (his cousin) in 1902, she took over the operation of the store. The Lees sold the ranch in 1913 and moved away but had to foreclose in 1919 so Agnes returned to running

Percheron team and sleigh with supplies at Lee's Grocery Store. Agnes "Gan Gan" Lee operated the store from 1919 until 1957. *Museum of the Cariboo Chilcotin, Williams Lake photo*

the store. When Norman died in 1939, she left the operation of the ranch in the hands of her son, Dan, and devoted her efforts to making the store the best it could. She had many friends among the Chilcotin Natives and could speak the Native language of Tsilhqot'in fluently. Although she had affectionately been called "Nessie" for years, her nickname changed when her grandchildren began calling her "Gan Gan." Soon everyone in the Chilcotin affectionately called her by that name. As Gan Gan got on in years, her eyesight began to fail and she had difficulty reading the numbers on the store scale, so she would instruct the customer to scoop the required amount into the tray. She also had a plate full of coins next to the cash register where customers could pick out their change. No one ever attempted to cheat her as she was considered one of the most trusted people in the entire Chilcotin. Mrs. Norman Lee, Gan Gan, operated the store until 1957 and died the next year at the age of 86.[26] By then the location of the store was referred to as Lee's Corner after the family.

For the larger ranches located far from even the smallest communities, it had always been necessary to bring in enough supplies to last for several months. So it was not surprising that many large ranches had their own general stores. This

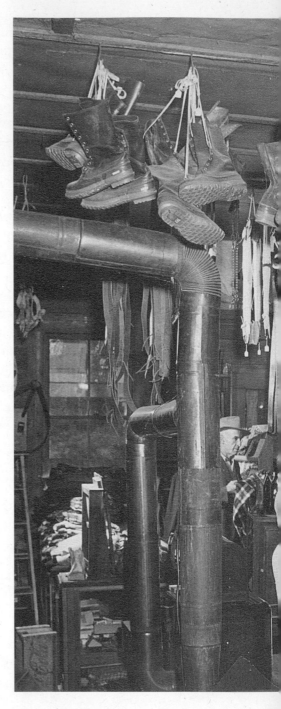

Ben and Joyce Jaffe wait on customers at the Chilco Ranch Store, 1950. The store boasted that it carried "everything from a needle to a wagon." *Museum of the Cariboo Chilcotin, Williams Lake photo*

let cowboys and their families obtain the best prices for all the clothing, supplies and groceries that they needed and eliminated the long drive to town to purchase necessities. The Chilco Ranch, situated on the south side of the Chilcotin River near Hanceville, was an excellent example. Opened in the 1930s, it stocked all the necessities, boasting that it carried "everything from a needle to a wagon."

> The store was always a fascinating place to enter. Clean and tidy and smelling of oranges, new saddle leather and buckskin gloves, mingled in winter with the fragrance of fir wood burning in the long barrel heater. It was warm and pleasant in the coldest weather, cool in summer, and was a jovial gathering place for the bunkhouse crew on most evenings. You could find anything there, from riding gear and harness to needles and thread; from cooking utensils and stoves to clothing and food. Most decorative was the stack of yard-square silk handkerchiefs piled on the wide varnished counter. Every colour of the rainbow was there, as well as black and white. Cowboys wound them around their necks and Indian women tied them on their heads. Almost every outdoors person wore one and considered it a treat to get a new silk handkerchief.[27]

Getting Together

Life on the ranches was not all hard work. There were opportunities to visit and socialize with friends and neighbours. People made their own fun and used whatever was at hand for entertainment. Every member of the community seemed to have some special talent that they would contribute to the mix. Some were musicians or singers, some experts in a certain subject; others had a particular skill such as juggling, telling stories or reciting poetry. When family and neighbours got together, everyone was expected to contribute something to the event. People would gather at a neighbour's house for a social time and often the whole neighbourhood would gather for a special event. During the summer months, picnics were a popular way for neighbours and families to get together. Pat Riley, who grew up at Dog Creek, remembered that her grandmother would get up at four in the morning to fry up the chicken and prepare the goodies for a picnic and daytrip to Dog Creek Mountain or Mineral Springs. For colder-weather gatherings, most communities had a schoolhouse that doubled as a hall where special events could be put on. Desks were mounted on runners so that they could easily be pushed to the side to make room for dancing or other activities such as club and political meetings.

The Graham family visiting neighbours at the Comer Ranch near Alexis Creek. On the isolated ranches, families packed onto a horse-drawn wagon and travelled for miles to visit neighbours.
Museum of the Cariboo Chilcotin, Williams Lake photo

As soon as a ranching community became large enough, people began to push for their own community hall. Most often the hall was financed by contributions from members of the community. This was the case in Grande Prairie (later re-named Westwold to avoid confusion with Alberta's Grande Prairie) where the Pringle family donated an acre of land and local residents purchased shares toward the construction. The Grande Prairie Assembly Hall was opened in 1900. It hosted six to eight dances every year and was used for political meetings and as a polling station on election day. The annual January masquerade was always a highlight of the year for residents. Rentals of the hall for weddings, dances and concerts always brought in enough income to provide janitorial and maintenance services. Despite the small profit made every year, it was agreed that the hall be sold by tender in 1911. It was sold for $500 with the stipulation that it should be kept in good condition for dancing and could be rented for that purpose. It seems that these stipulations were passed down from owner to owner, as the hall was still being used for dances in the late 1930s. Eventually the hall became a cow barn, and in 1938, the community decided to construct the new Westwold Community Hall. Unfortunately, construction on the new hall was interrupted by the war and it remained a shell until after 1945.

In Big Bar, the community got together to build a log community hall for dances, church services, elections and political meetings whenever the local elected official would pay a rare visit to his constituency. Harry Marriott described the dances:

> The dances were more or less always colourful affairs, lively and full of ginger and snap amongst the young folks. Many of the Big Bar boys were natural-born fiddlers, and the girls were all darn good dancers. The sight of these good-looking half-breed gals all tucked out in smart Timothy Eaton dresses with their hair all decorated up with bright coloured ribbons, just looked like water in the desert to an active snoozer of a half-lonesome cowboy. Many romances were started, and some finished, around that Community Hall. Just outside the hall were some thick willows and cottonwood trees close to the creek and these provided an all-out setting, so necessary and important to the privacy required for successful courting. One of the local boys must have been reading some of Bill Shakespeare's plays at some time, as he christened this quiet little spot "The Bridge of Sighs."[28]

As there was very little real cash around Big Bar in the 1930s, the young bucks couldn't afford store-bought liquor but there was an excellent local version of moonshine made from yeast cakes, potatoes, raisins and sugar. Needless to say, with this concoction fuelling the boys, a few fights would break out on occasion and out-and-out brawls were not unheard of. In fact, fights became so common at the Big Creek Community Hall that it earned a bad reputation and became known as the Howling Dog Dance Hall.

By contrast, religion was a focal point of activities in many communities as the settlers depended upon the faith of their fathers to sustain them through difficult times. Herbert Edward Church was a mud pup who came to the Chilcotin in the early 1900s and settled at Big Creek. His wife, Gertrude, was a devout Anglican and must have taken her married name seriously as she was instrumental in having a church constructed at Big Creek. The Church of St. James was built on land donated by her husband and was completed in 1931 with stained glass windows, rich brocade hangings, intricate hand-carvings and a varnished floor! Gertrude lovingly kept the church clean and decorated it for the monthly services, for which she played the organ. Appropriately, the first wedding to take place in the little church was that of the Churches' son Dick. The Churches also contributed land for the construction of a large hall adjoining the church and the two buildings were the heart of the Big Creek community.

Christianity was the dominant religion in ranching country, and there was little denominational division. Settlers were happy to have a church service to attend, regardless of their denomination. Given the large number of settlers from Britain, it is not surprising that the Anglican Church was well represented. Canon Akehurst arrived in Kamloops in the early years of the century and was appointed rector of a territory that covered about 6,000 square miles. He travelled about his "parish" and held services in people's homes and never turned anyone away, even if they were not of the Anglican persuasion. He was a welcome sight wherever he travelled.

> Canon Akehurst and his fat little pony used to travel in the summer over these roads and trails, holding services, baptising all the new arrivals and holding weddings or funerals as needed. That same fat little pony was quite a celebrity and the old man's first consideration; he always insisted on looking after and stabling him without any help. There seemed to be a mutual understanding between them; at the foot of any incline on the road, the pony would stop. The old man, in frock and gaiters, would get out of the two-wheeled cart and, with the pony pulling a little and the sky pilot pushing a lot, they would eventually reach the top of the hill and go on their way rejoicing.[29]

During the 1930s, another regular sight throughout the Cariboo was the Ford van with lettering on the side reading "Sunday School Mission—Anglican Church Cariboo Diocese." Inside were two women who travelled the country instructing children in the Christian faith, regardless of denomination. The women had undergone rigorous examination before being accepted for this gruelling undertaking. They even had to have a doctor's certificate, which, among other things, certified that the candidate's digestion was strong. The vans, which were fitted for a spartan existence, operated in spring, summer and fall, during which time the women visited isolated rural areas to start Sunday schools, visit homes, teach Vacation Bible School, recruit members for Sunday school by mail, inform clergymen of children needing baptism and, where no ministers were available, conduct services. The Cariboo Diocese assumed responsibility for running the vans and for providing living expenses to the women. Each spring the "Vanners," as they were called, were given a "can shower" where one Sunday was set aside for the congregation to bring canned goods for the women. One year, a van departed with no fewer than 50 cans of sardines! The ladies usually had their supply of canned food supplemented by local produce from ranch families.

Sports in ranching country usually consisted of baseball in the summer and hockey in the winter. Communities would have their own teams that could challenge surrounding areas in these games and everyone would turn out to watch. In the Kamloops area, Sullivan Valley, Branhartvale, Kamloops, Savona, Tranquille and Beresford all had "athletic clubs" that would organize sporting events, and sponsor picnics, corn roasts and dances as well.

At Dog Creek, the new school teacher in 1929 was Doreen Pollitt. She had grown up in Peace River country where hockey flourished and she encouraged her students to give it a try. There was no shortage of frozen meadows and creeks, so, before long, all the young people in the area were struggling along on skates and banging a frozen horse bun for a puck. Their hockey equipment was primitive at best, consisting of magazines for shin guards and stripped willow branches for sticks. It wasn't long until the enthusiastic youngsters graduated to real rubber pucks and factory-made sticks, but their hockey gloves were still Native-made buckskin gauntlets that served the purpose well. The local Native kids played as well, most of them having learned to skate at the Residential School at 150 Mile House. They loved the game and delighted in the thrill of skating at top speed down the ice and stick-handling around their opponents.

Among the many teams of Native players in the Cariboo, one rose to the top. Alkali Lake's appropriately named Alkali Lake Braves formed in 1927, at a time when there was no Cariboo Hockey League, just a mix of teams from Clinton to Prince George, that included the reserves of Sugar Cane, Canim Lake and Alkali Lake. The Alkali Lake team was not exactly flush. They had no money to travel to games or to eat when they were visiting another team. The team would often make the 35-mile trip to Williams Lake, travelling by horse and sleigh, with frozen deer meat and potatoes for food. The team of six or seven players and their fans travelled in a caravan of three sleighs and several saddle horses for 10 to 12 hours to Williams Lake. Natives were not allowed in the hotels in Williams Lake, so the team had to spend their nights sleeping in tents beside the rink. Since there were so few players, most of the Braves played the entire game.

Charles E. Wynn-Johnson, who owned the Alkali Lake Ranch, decided to help the Braves out and purchased green uniforms for them. In return, some of the players helped Wynn-Johnson with haying in the summer time. Shin pads were made out of buckskin and willow sticks and padded with deer hair. Skates were sharpened by hand with a file and stone and were patched with buckskin and laced with rawhide. Captain Laurie Wilson, Wynn-Johnson's son-in-law, agreed to organize and manage the team with the help of Harry Taylor, the Indian Agent at Williams Lake. The first game the Braves played was against Lac la Hache, considered to be the powerhouse in the league. The Braves played extremely well and were only edged out by a score of 2 to 1.

That was all that was needed to give the players the confidence that they could compete with any team in the league.

By the time the 1930–31 season rolled around, the Braves were an experienced team and recognized not only as one of the best but also one of the cleanest teams in the Cariboo. They easily handled every team they played that season and finally defeated perennial champion Prince George to take the league title. With Matthew Dick in goal, Joe Clemine and David Johnson on defence, Pat Chelsea and Alfred Sandy on the wings, and Alec Antoine, known as Sylista, at centre, they prevailed over all-comers. Sylista was the star of the Braves and, every time the team needed a goal, he would score.

The Alkali Lake Braves were formed in 1927, at a time when there was no Cariboo Hockey League. Pictured are (left to right): Joe Clemene, Patrick Chelsea, Matthew Dick, Joe Dan, David Johnson, Alec Antoine, Louis Emile, Peter Christopher and Alfred Sandy. Vancouver Sun *photo. Copy courtesy of Laura Johnson, Andy Chelsea and Liz Twan.*

As the Northern BC champions, the Braves were invited by Andy Paull, president of the North American Indian Brotherhood to play against an all-star commercial team in the Vancouver Forum in a two-game series. Most of the team had never been to Vancouver and the sight of all the tall buildings left them wide-eyed. But they were undaunted for their performance on the ice. It was a new experience to play on such a large, artificial ice surface and, even more surprising, in a rink with boards! In the Cariboo, most rinks were banked with snow. The Braves played a total of nine men, which allowed little room for substitution, but they were a hit with the fans, drawing 8,000 people to each game. They lost two close games, 2 to 1 and 1 to 0, but won the hearts of the fans. The Vancouver newspapers were full of pictures and articles about them. After the games, the legendary Lester Patrick offered Sylista a chance to play professionally but he turned it down. "I've got a good job at Alkali Lake Ranch," he said, not mentioning that it paid $15 a month. Sylista was born a Tsilhqot'in but had been brought up at Alkali Lake. He was built heavier and stronger

and was a more determined competitor than his Secwepemc (Shuswap) teammates. None of the other Braves would hurt another player to win, but Sylista would. The following year saw an example of his grit.

In 1931–32, the Braves met a team from the new mining town of Wells in the championships. This team was made up of big, mean prairie farm boys and had played its way to the finals through physical intimidation. Their meanest player, Red Waller, soon realized that Sylista was the Braves' best player and set out to put him out of the game. He hit Sylista with a vicious two-hander to the foot, breaking three bones in the arch. A doctor at the game examined Sylista and ordered him to the hospital. Sylista refused and returned to the ice. When he got the puck next, he fired a shot that "accidentally" caught Waller on the side of the head. It took a week in hospital for Waller to be able to function again and, not surprisingly, the Braves won the championship.

Chilco Ranch main house. Cousins Spencer formed the Chilco Ranch from a number of smaller ranches in 1923. *Museum of the Cariboo Chilcotin, Williams Lake photo*

By the 1932–33 season, the Braves were in tough financial shape. They continued to patch up their green uniforms and travel to games but that year they lost the championship to Prince George by one goal. After that, their manager, Captain Wilson, decided to return to the east and, lacking a coach and manager, the team quietly folded. In the few years that they had played together the Alkali Lake Braves had become a legend.

The Two Spencers

Cousins Spencer

Cousins Spencer was an English Canadian who purchased the Bell, Scallon, Vedan, Wilson, Davy, Allan, Deer Creek and A1 ranches and formed the

Chilco Ranch in 1923. This gave him more than a million acres of deeded land, leases and grazing permits. He could afford these acquisitions, having made a fortune in the motion picture industry in Australia. Spencer used his good business sense to operate the ranch effectively. Although he was not interested in getting his hands dirty with ranch work, preferring to dress in a suit and vest, he was certainly businesslike. He opened a large store at the ranch and offered a wide variety of goods. It was Spencer who coined the phrase "Everything from a needle to a wagon." Unfortunately, his preoccupation with making a dollar tended to make him hard-nosed and he soon gained the reputation of being tight-fisted and unneighbourly. By contrast, his wife, Mary Stuart, was generous and friendly and helped to offset Spencer's offensiveness.

By 1930, Spencer was showing signs of stress and had started acting in a strange and unpredictable manner. Things came to a head in September of that year. He asked his foreman, Dave Stoddart, and bookkeeper, Ed Smith, to drive with him on business to the Deer Creek cabin, located on an isolated part of the ranch. Spencer had brought his shotgun along in case they encountered a grouse on the way. Once they had completed their business, Smith turned to lock the cabin door and Spencer shot him in the back with the shotgun. Then he turned to his foreman and shot at him, hitting him in the arm. Spencer turned and walked away, leaving the two men lying bleeding on the ground. Stoddart struggled to get a tourniquet on his bleeding arm and then tried to help Smith, who was obviously dying. Stoddart tried to start back in the ranch truck but, between the loss of blood and fear that Spencer would return, he got stuck and had to hide in a ditch. It was some time before Mrs. Spencer and the ranch carpenter, Christopher Vick, became concerned that the men were overdue and drove to the cabin. There they found Stoddart and Smith's body. Stoddart was rushed to hospital in Williams Lake and the police were alerted.

The police dispatched a constable who, along with Rene Hance, on his first assignment as a coroner, to bring in Smith's body. When they got to the scene of the crime it was dark and they could see the dead body in the pouring rain. Fearful that Spencer was still around, they surveyed the grisly scene in the headlights. The policemen asked Hance, "Well, you are the coroner, what do you want to do?" Rene replied, "I want to resign." They brought out the body and a search for the killer began. For two months, Spencer could not be found and the ranch cowboys went around armed at all times. Finally a Chilcotin Native tracker, Little Charlie, found his body under a log-jam in the Chilcotin River, with the shotgun not far away. It appeared that Spencer had tried to cross the river and had been swept under the log-jam. A handsome reward was paid to Little Charlie and compensation to Smith's estate and to Stoddart, who lost his arm. Spencer left an estate of $500,000 and the Chilco Ranch was debt-free. A few years later, Christopher Vick married Mary Stuart and the two sold the ranch in 1937.[30]

Colonel Victor Spencer

Victor Spencer was born in Victoria in 1882. His father, David, was by then a successful dry goods merchant, eventually owning nine stores. Victor went off to fight in the Boer War in 1900 and, when the First World War broke out, he enlisted again and fought in France, eventually rising to the rank of colonel. In the early 1920s, Spencer purchased the Earlscourt Ranch near Lytton and began raising purebred Hereford bulls. A man of tireless energy, he was active in business, investing in the Pioneer Gold Mine, which later amalgamated with Bralorne, and also encouraging the start of the BC honey industry. In 1936, at the height of the Depression, the David Spencer Department Store Ltd. operated department stores in Victoria, Nanaimo, Vancouver, Chilliwack and New Westminster. David Spencer Department Store purchased the historic Pavilion Ranch near Lillooet and the Meason Ranch on Little Dog Creek in the South Cariboo. The Meason Ranch was renamed the Diamond S, which was the logo for the department stores. The company had bought the ranches so that it could have a steady supply of beef for its stores. Victor Spencer became actively involved in setting up the ranch and was a regular visitor. To stock the Diamond S Ranch, he purchased 1,000 head of cattle in Alberta. Spencer had the Alberta cattle shipped by rail to Agassiz in the Fraser Valley where they were loaded into the company's furniture delivery vans to be trucked to the CPR. This may have been the first example of trucking cattle in British Columbia. Nothing was recorded about the condition of the delivery vans after they were used as cattle liners. The cattle were then loaded into cattle cars and travelled by rail to Ashcroft. There they were met by Frank Armes, the new ranch manager, with a group of cowboys and a chuckwagon and driven to Dog Creek. Much of the first part of the drive was on the highway and had to take place early in the morning before traffic became too heavy. The Diamond S eventually ran over 3,000 head of Herefords and Victor Spencer used the most modern ranching methods he could. He brought in his purebred Hereford bulls from the Earlscourt Ranch for breeding to keep his bloodlines pure. He practised effective rangeland management and a large percentage of his cows produced calves so that the finest prime beef cattle could be slaughtered for the Spencer department stores' meat departments.

Branding in the Okanagan Valley. This early branding scene shows the mixed-breed cattle that dominated before the Hereford breed became popular. *Vernon Museum and Archives photo*

Branding crew on Moon Ranch, 1942. Branding gave the young boys a chance to work with the men. *Museum of the Cariboo Chilcotin, Williams Lake photo*

Colonel Spencer left the actual operation of the ranch in the capable hands of Frank Armes, preferring to use the ranch for hunting and fishing. He brought a steady stream of influential guests to see the ranch and to shoot birds on the lakes of Dog Creek Mountain. Spencer's favourite meal was a whole mallard and roasted corn on the cob from the ranch garden. Harry Chamberlain, David Spencer Department Store's manager, and his family were frequent visitors to the ranch as well.[31]

Branding was a big event on the ranch. Joe Labourdais, whose father, Ed, had a small ranch on nearby Keller Lake, never missed an opportunity to get involved.

The Diamond S Ranch would have a branding day on Pavilion Mountain one day in the spring. It would be a two hour ride from Keller Lake where I lived to the corrals on the mountain. As soon as they got enough calf wrestlers they would start branding. There were twelve calf wrestlers, six teams of two. I'd grab the calf's head when it came to the fire and flip it and then hold one front leg. My partner would hold one hind leg and stretch it out. There was a guy who would cut, another dehorn, another give shots and another brand. A bunch of the girls would be working giving shots, dehorning, and tallying. It would take a little over three hours to do seven hundred head of calves. After the branding there would be beer and juice and a big feast. The cooks would roast beef and sweetbreads over an open fire. The sweetbreads would have the skin taken off them and fired in butter on four big pancake griddles.[32]

In the early 1950s, the management of the Diamond S was turned over to Victor Spencer's daughter, Barbara, who promptly rechristened the ranch the Circle S. She turned the ranch over to her brother, Victor Jr., who operated it into the 1960s. Victor spearheaded the establishment of the BC Lions football team in 1953 and is a member of the Canadian Football Hall of Fame.

Chapter Four

WINDS OF WAR

Canada officially declared war on Germany on September 10, 1939. Most people believed initially that the war would be a short and inexpensive one, but when the Allies were defeated in Belgium and France in 1940, that idea went straight out the window. As the entire country mobilized, the demand for commodities grew and beef prices rose rapidly. The high demand for beef in Canada, Britain and the United States kept prices on the rise and, for the first time in a decade, there was real competition for cattle. Burns and Swifts found themselves in competition with each other and with smaller companies, as well as commission agencies like Weiller and Williams Limited, whose Edmonton partner, Lee Williams, would purchase and send BC cattle to buyers all across the continent in the years to come.

While the price of beef soared, much to the beleaguered ranchers' delight, the availability of manpower on the ranches plummeted as thousands of young men joined up and went off to fight the war. Wages had to go up to attract labour from the diminishing numbers of available men, which meant that profits went down. Despite the difficult labour market, the BC government saw fit to prohibit the hiring of labour from outside of the province, which also forced wages up and further reduced manpower availability. Alex Bulman of the Willow Ranch referred to the problem and the ranchers' response. "In the fall of '39 when the storm broke, there was a loss of men to the armed forces . . . We were finally down to a couple of men at Westwold and the Willow. It was only due to mechanization, primitive as it then was, that we were able to carry on at all." [1]

Prince Domino, grand champion at the Kamloops bull sale in 1934, showing a fresh Douglas Lake "111" brand. It is unlikely that the nose ring would have been left in once the bull was turned out on the range. *Doug Cox photo*

As the war dragged on, the Canadian government became worried that too many Canadian cattle were being sold across the border in the United States. In 1942, it imposed an embargo on exporting cattle to the US. This deprived the ranchers of their bargaining power and weakened the market. The government also imposed a ceiling on cattle prices, which ate even further into the profits. To make matters worse, beef was rationed to two pounds per person a week. This encouraged consumers, especially in British Columbia, to purchase only the highest-grade cuts of beef and made the lower grades difficult to sell. And, with the war effort commanding most of the available train cars, freighting cattle to the eastern markets became more expensive.

Ranchers grudgingly accepted the factors that limited their newfound profits, knowing that the war effort required everyone in Canada to make sacrifices. But they were an enterprising lot and they looked for other ways to make a dollar. At the Douglas Lake Ranch, new manager Brian Chance decided to go into hogs, something that might have seemed anathema to the early ranchers. He had ranch workers construct a large piggery at Chaperon Lake and brought in 90 brood sows, each of which would farrow twice a year. Once the piglets were weaned, they were fed grain from the Prairies. Fattening them up in this way was made economical by the federal government's temporary Freight Assistance Policy that covered the cost of shipping grain from the Prairies for the purpose of finishing livestock. When they were six months old, the pigs were shipped to Swifts Canadian Company for butchering. An estimated 400 Douglas Lake hog carcasses a year, valued at $10,000, were sent to Britain each year to feed the armed forces. An additional 150 carcasses fed the ranch staff and neighbouring purchasers.

Swifts Canadian Company regularly tested hogs for a variety of diseases and, in two instances, traces of tuberculosis showed up in the organs of the Douglas Lake hogs. The first time, the Dominion health inspectors condemned only the organs of the hogs and deemed the rest of the carcasses acceptable, having tested negative for the disease. When traces of TB were found in another batch of hogs, Chance brought in the provincial veterinarian Dr. Wallace Gunn who, before he even entered the facility, spotted the problem. Hundreds of pigeons were flying into and nesting at the Home Ranch. Dr. Gunn recommended total elimination of the pigeons that were carrying avian TB. When former manager Frank Ward and his shooting friends came up for hunting season, they gleefully agreed to look after the extermination. Four hundred of the winged enemies fell on the first day alone and, before the avid shooters were done, the problem was eliminated.[2]

Cayuses

By the 1940s, there were scores of horses on the ranges of the British Columbia Interior. Though many of these were owned by horse ranchers, they mixed freely with the wild horses that had proliferated on the unfenced ranges. In BC, the wild horses were generally known as "cayuses," a term unknown in the south or east of the Rockies. It came from the Cayuse Native people in eastern Washington and Oregon who were noted for their expert horsemanship and careful breeding of these small, strong horses. The term came north with the early drovers and miners and came to refer to any wild horse that could be broken for ranch work. Cayuses were particularly adapted to surviving in the harsh northern climate, being capable of surviving all but the toughest winters because of their ability to scratch in the snow for the grasses underneath. As long as there was grass beneath the snow, these horses could paw with their front feet to get at it. Cattle could not do this. They had to push through the snow with their noses and could not handle as much snow as horses. A thaw followed by freezing temperatures would leave cattle struggling to push through the crust. Horses therefore had a distinct advantage over cattle, which had to be fed hay once the winter snow had fallen.

Because of this advantage, raising horses had always been seen as an inexpensive way to get into the ranching business. All that was required was a good stud horse and a few mares. Once or twice a year ranchers would round up the horses and drive them into corrals where they could be branded and sorted. The good horses would be separated out for ranch use or sale and the remaining ones turned loose on the range again as breeding stock or until needed again. Horse ranching was particularly popular among the Native people of the province who seldom had enough capital to purchase a herd of cattle. Natives were not allowed to own their own land, however, and had to restrict themselves to reserve land or take their chances turning cattle or horses loose on Crown land.

Year after year ranchers had brought their cattle in for the winter, leaving the horses on the range to fend for themselves. As a result, when the grass began to grow in the spring, the horses would immediately begin grazing, keeping the grass cropped close to the ground and leaving little for the cattle when they were turned loose on the range. The first six weeks of growth in the spring were crucial for the grasses, many of which were delicate and susceptible to overgrazing, especially in these early weeks. Most of the rangeland was leased to the ranchers by the government and cattle ranchers had to have a grazing permit every summer to turn their cattle loose on

Crown land. The same applied to horse ranchers but they seldom bothered to apply for permits, much to the disgust of cattle ranchers.

Things came to a head in the early 1940s, when the multitude of horses on the ranges had become a problem. The cattle ranchers were resentful because they had to pay yearly grazing fees and most horse ranchers did not, even though their horses grazed for 12 months a year. For a long time, the government had ignored the problem because it could not impound the horses and sell them to recover grazing fees whereas they certainly could impound cattle and sell them for a profit. Only after years of protesting and lobbying by the cattle ranchers did the government take action by instituting a policy that paid $5 for every unbranded horse that was shot on the ranges. The shooters had to bring in the scalp and ears of the horse to receive payment. As might be expected, since all the shooters had to bring in were the ears and scalp, many branded horses were shot in the process, making horse ranchers very unhappy. Tensions between the horse ranchers and cattle ranchers grew.

The government called meetings in each of the ranching areas to allow the parties to bring their grievances before each other. A meeting at the Spences Bridge schoolhouse was typical of those held at the time. Ranchers arrived in their worn-out cars and trucks and the Natives arrived on saddle horses or with teams and buggies. The local forest ranger was in charge of the meeting and outlined the problem. The horses were eating around 80 acres of grass each, compared to the cattle that were consuming about 40 acres of grass during the six-month grazing season. The cattlemen had to pay grazing fees while the horse ranchers were getting away with paying nothing. The ranger said the government would pay the sum of $5 for every horse shot or delivered to them. This offer looked fair to the cattle ranchers and the cowboys who could make money on the process but the older horse ranchers, most of them Native, were more sceptical. The old Native ranchers sat in silence with their arms folded across their chest and, every once in a while, would let out a low guttural sound that sounded like "umpah." After the forest ranger had had his say, the local preacher rose to encourage the crowd to accept the new policy. He exhorted the men to work together for the good of all and, in eloquent language, told the Natives to accept the government offer. His somewhat condescending attitude to the Native elders came to a head when he referred to them as "God's children of the ranges," to which the old men again replied, "Umpah." As he rambled on, he felt that he was scoring points with the Native elders and that "umpah" was a sound of approval. After the meeting, he was walking by the spot where the Natives had tethered their horses when one of the young Natives warned him, "Careful, Reverend, not to step into some umpah."[3]

The new government policy spurred many cowboys into action. The ranchers were prepared to pay $5 a head for their branded horses that they couldn't otherwise catch. The cowboys could sell the unbranded ones to the fox-meat buyers or the government, which would pay $5 for every horse removed from the range. Any way you looked at it, there was money to be made. But the horses were wild and not easily caught. They were as wary as deer and just as fast, so the best time to catch them was in the winter when snow and scanty feed slowed them down. Cowboys would ride quietly through the area where they believed there was a bunch of horses, being careful not to make any noise or talk to each other. By the time they came across horse tracks, the herd was probably already running. The cowboys on their well-fed horses would run the wild horses, 10 to 40 at a time, for miles in the deep snow. Gradually they would be worked toward a corral with wings to funnel the horses in.

Francis Haller and Joe Lebourdais worked together during the early years of the Second World War catching wild horses in the south Cariboo. There were dozens of wild horse corrals in the 70 Mile, 83 Mile, Duckfoot Mountain and Big Bar areas of the Cariboo. They had been built years earlier and were used and maintained by generations of horse catchers. The heavy log corrals were 30 to 40 feet across and built with a gate that would drop with the pull of a rope. The walls were 10 feet high but, even at that height, some horses would do their best to climb the walls. As soon as the cowboys got the herd into the corral, one would reach up and yank the rope that tripped the drop gate shut. The cowboys would leave the horses in the corral for a couple of days and Francis Haller would walk through them to find out which horses were the leaders. He would rope a horse by the forefeet and throw it down and then do the same to one of the leaders. The two horses would be tied neck-to-neck, allowing them a little room to move. At first the horses would fight to get apart, but before long they would get used to being tied together. With the leaders under control in this way, cowboys could lead the pair of tied horses out of the corral at a slow lope and the entire herd would follow. Another cowboy would follow behind and keep the herd together as they travelled to the nearest stockyards or ranch corral where they could be sold. Good saddle horses or workhorses would sell for $10 once they were broken.

The alternative of rounding up horses and selling the good ones for use in farm work like haying and grain growing was much more acceptable to ranchers, but the increasing number of tractors on farms and ranches was gradually displacing horses as the source of power. However, occasionally there were other options for wild horse catchers. In the south Okanagan, several men worked for Paul White, who had been an engineer on the Grand

Coulee Dam and had landed the contract to supply horses to the US Cavalry. Ed Lacey, Wally Lindstrom and one of the McLeans travelled up and down the Okanagan and Similkameen valleys and purchased horses, offering anything from $5 to $10 a horse. They would travel as far as Kamloops looking for quiet mounts. They would drop by the local bars with cash in their pockets and talk to the cowboys and Natives, who would be happy to receive some cash. Later in the contract, Lacey would get a phone call that a carload of wild horses collected by independent horse catchers was coming to Oliver at the end of the rail line.

When the horses were gathered, the cowboys would bring them down through the reserve to Lacey's parents' ranch near Osoyoos, where they would be kept in corrals. Each cowboy would pick a horse that looked calm and ride it until it was gentle. The cowboys used a snaffle bit to work the horse as it had to be completely calm and manageable to be accepted by the cavalry. They would have to be able to pick up each foot in turn and curry comb the horse front and back.

From Osoyoos, every six weeks about 75 horses would be driven down the highway to the old stockyards just across the border in Tonasket, Washington, where the cavalry headquarters were. The colonel in charge would have a channel ploughed out in the winter so that he could run the horses through and test them for gentleness. Each cowboy would each have about 10 horses to look after. One at a time, the cowboys would ride a horse out and back at a walk, then a trot and then at a gallop as men on either side of them would beat the ground with whips to try and spook it. If the horse reacted too much it was immediately disqualified and taken back to the corral. But horses that were accepted would bring the cowboys $175 a head. Not a bad return on investment! Over the winter of 1939–40, Lacey and his cowboys bought about 400 head of horses in Canada and sold them across the line in Tonasket.[4]

Innovators

Dick Church: The Big Creek Ranching Company

The Big Creek Ranching Company was started when Herbert Edmond Church pre-empted 320 acres of land in the Big Creek area in 1903. The ranch was operated for the next 30 years by H.E. Church and his family and it was H.E. who had the idea of keeping a few head of milk cows in order to sell butter to the mines around the Chilcotin. He sold some of his beef cattle and invested in milk cows from the Fraser Valley, then purchased a big combined

Cattle drive near Williams Lake. By the 1940s, Herefords were becoming the dominant breed of cattle in the BC Interior. *Museum of the Cariboo Chilcotin, Williams Lake photo*

churn and butter worker, with a gas motor to run it, and a cream vat. The next year, he sold $1,500 worth of butter; in the years to come, up to 4,000 pounds of butter were sold from his small herd of dairy cows.

H.E. was not the only member of the family to think outside the box. Some time before H.E's death in 1933, his son Dick took over running the ranch and eventually ran 500 head of cattle. Dick Church was a man with progressive ideas about operating a ranch. He hired more men and seeded pasture to hay land, using commercial fertilizer to increase production. He bought a hammer mill to chop the hay and make it more economical to feed to cattle and horses and he even trucked in grain to finish the cattle. This made his cattle very attractive to buyers and kept his income steady through the 1930s. Dick brought in horses from Alberta and purchased a quarter horse stallion, Easy Money, for breeding. Soon his saddle horses were commanding top dollar as well.

Always on the lookout for good summer grazing, Dick convinced his neighbour Gerald Blenkinsop that they should drive steers over the mountains and graze them on the western slope. In the summer of 1938, they drove a herd up Big Creek to Graveyard Valley and over Elbow Pass to the lush bunchgrass hills around Spruce Lake, not far from Bridge River. They left one rider to stay with the cattle through the summer and, in the fall, drove the cattle to Shalalth on the PGE Railway where they could be shipped to Vancouver. In 1939, Blenkinsop decided not to carry on with the experiment, but Dick continued for another five years. The story goes that when scientists suggested there might be grass on the moon, neighbour Charlie Erickson quickly responded, "Don't tell Dick Church. He'll be trying to take his steers up there."[5]

Dick was instrumental in the establishment of the Big Creek Livestock Association and was president from its beginning in the 1930s until shortly before his death in 1975. In this capacity, he convinced the government to allow spring turn-outs of cattle along the Chilcotin River for Big Creek cattle. He also had a TD9 caterpiller tractor that he hired out for road building and for the construction of the Puntzi Lake airstrip. He operated a sawmill on his ranch and by the 1950s he was cutting lumber commercially.

Dick Church, like his father, H.E., was a man of vision and foresight. Although he never made a fortune from his various ventures, he is remembered as a man who was not afraid to try new things.

Charles Cowan: The Onward Ranch

The Onward Ranch, just eight miles south of Williams Lake, was established in 1867 by Charles Boromeo Eagle, of Pennsylvanian Dutch extraction, who pre-empted land along the San Jose River. He named his ranch Onward

The Onward ranch house was built in 1886 and renovated by John Edward Moore during the First World War. *Museum of the Cariboo Chilcotin, Williams Lake photo*

because he felt it would always progress and move onward. Even in those early days, Eagle was not afraid to try new things. He constructed seven miles of irrigation ditch, which carried water from a permanent supply. With this abundance of water, Eagle grew as much as 225,000 pounds of grain, 250,000 pounds of vegetables and 200 tons of hay annually. His produce won medals in Canada and Europe. The Onward was sold in 1903 to John Edgar Moore, who also owned the Alkali Lake Ranch. Moore reopened the store that had been operated by the Eagle family, refurbished the lovely ranch house that had been built in 1886 and made the Onward into a going concern. In 1920, Moore sold the ranch to Charles G. Cowan and his wife, Vivian, of Kamloops.

John Edward Moore, who also owned the Alkali Lake Ranch, bought the Onward Ranch in 1903 and made it a going concern. *Museum of the Cariboo Chilcotin, Williams Lake photo*

Charles Cowan was born in Dublin, Ireland, and moved to South Carolina at the age of 15. After that he joined the North West Mounted Police and served with them for six years. He then became a big-game hunter and guide, earning the nickname "Dead-eye Dick" in the English newspapers. As a guide, he got to know members of the British aristocracy, whom he encouraged to invest in the Cariboo. He convinced the Marquis of Exeter to buy large tracts of land around and including 100 Mile House at the same time as Lord Egerton of Tatton purchased the 105, 108 and 111 Mile ranches. Cowan was appointed to oversee their holdings until, in 1930, the Marquis of Exeter's son, Lord Martin Cecil, took over.

When Cowan took over the Onward Ranch it needed major improvements. Eagle and Moore had grown grain for such a long time without fertilizing that the soil was in poor condition, so he concentrated on "bringing back the land" by sowing the fields with legume crops and then ploughing them under. He also fertilized the land heavily and added miles of irrigation ditches as well as cleaning out the old ones. His land-reclamation project was successful, and the Onward began to grow quality crops again. Cowan added the nearby 150 Mile Ranch to his holdings in 1929 and practised the same revitalization program on its fields. Because he was in poor health, Cowan appointed John Zirnhelt to run the ranches and moved to Victoria. In 1939, he suffered a massive stroke and died. Vivian returned to the Onward and founded the Cariboo Art Society to encourage young artists. She sold the ranch in 1966.[6]

Lord Martin Cecil: 100 Mile House

In 1930, a 21-year-old Englishman, Martin Cecil, arrived at the small settlement of 100 Mile House after a five-hour drive along the dusty Cariboo Road. On viewing the dilapidated huddle of buildings that housed the dozen inhabitants of the town, his heart sank. What had he gotten himself into?

Lord Martin Cecil, whose father was the fifth Marquis of Exeter, was born in 1909 at Burghley House, a modest dwelling of some 200-plus rooms. The rundown shacks of 100 Mile must have seemed a long way from his roots. His father had purchased the 15,000-acre Bridge Creek Ranch, which surrounded the 100 Mile House, in 1912 and Lord Cecil, after three years in the Royal Navy, agreed to run it. His first task was to construct a reasonable habitation to replace the decrepit roadhouse. He had no experience in construction but, armed with some books on construction methods and with the help of a few local men, he designed and built the 100 Mile Lodge. He even devised a plumbing system for the new building, using a flume that brought water from Bridge Creek into a 1,000-gallon holding tank above the lodge. This system had its obvious limitations in that the water in the flume froze solid during the lengthy Cariboo winter, necessitating the hauling of water from the creek. Cecil also brought in and installed a 32-volt electrical system.

Cecil also took over the running of the Highland Ranch, owned by Lord Ederton of Tatton, bringing a total of 50,000 acres under his control. A good judge of character, he hired Alex Morrison to run the 100 Mile Lodge and Don Laidlaw to run the Highland Ranch. As the Depression descended on the BC Interior, Cecil faced an overwhelming challenge: how to keep the huge holdings under his oversight from disappearing in debt. Between them, the two ranches had 2,000 head of cattle and an equal number of sheep, none of them worth much. Cecil decided that the sheep were less valuable than the cattle and sold them off or traded them for hay. As he began to understand the cattle industry, he became more involved in the political end of the system. When the Cariboo Stockmen's Association was formed in 1934, Cecil became vice-president. The following year, he worked closely with George Mayfield in forming a co-operative marketing system that kept the cattle auctions in the hands of the ranchers. That led to the establishment of the Cariboo Cattlemen's Association in 1943, with Cecil as its first president. He was also very involved in the small 100 Mile community as the postmaster and

Imperial Oil agent. A deeply spiritual man, Cecil established an Emissaries of Divine Light chapter at 100 Mile and was very involved in the leadership of the international movement.

Lord Cecil Martin looked every inch the working rancher with his casual shirt, jeans and cowboy hat, even when he became the Seventh Marquis of Exeter in 1981. In this position, he had to travel to Westminster to take his seat in the House of Lords. But his home remained 100 Mile House until his death in 1988.[7]

Tough Characters

The cowboy has had a reputation for toughness since the beginning of the cattle industry in North America. Anyone who spends his life in the outdoors far from the niceties of civilization needs to be prepared for hardship and the cowboy epitomizes the image of the rugged individual. But even among those who earned this reputation for toughness, there were some who stood out. They were men and women who knew hardship and isolation and rose above those challenges by not only persevering but also excelling in a life that many would find impossible.

Joe Coutlee

The year 1945 saw the death of a legend: Joe Coutlee, who had been cow boss at the Douglas Lake Ranch since 1896. Coutlee was affectionately known to his cowboys as Roaring Bill because of his reputed ability to wake the dead with his booming voice. He was a cowboy's cowboy, able to ride any horse, break the meanest bronco, rope with the best of them, handle a gun and handle the toughest weather. As cow boss, he could read the range and know how many head of cattle a given field would support and for how long. He was a large man, six feet tall and weighing 200 pounds, and could handle himself in a fight. When there was work to be done, he was all business, but when work was over he indulged in drinking bouts that were the stuff of legends. He was larger than life in many ways and those who had worked for him would say with pride for the rest of their life, "I rode for Coutlee."

Once during a slow time, when the liquor had been flowing for a few days, he decided to head back to the home ranch on a wagon driven by "Whistling Tex" Turner. Like many Texans, Turner was not backward in promoting the Lone Star State as the biggest and the best and he would punctuate his glowing promotion of Texas by cracking his whip over his team. Coutlee was justifiably proud of his native country and not at all impressed by the whip cracking. When his notoriously short fuse had reached explosion point with Turner's antics, he jumped up, threw down the reins and whipped the team into a mad gallop. The wagon and its contents careened down the road and into a gully, shattering into pieces. Coutlee didn't fare much better than the wagon. One of his ears had to be sewn back on, but at least he had shown this Texan how Canadians drove horses.

On another occasion, Coutlee was heading back from Merritt to the Courtney Lake cow camp on a cold November day. As was his practice, he had a sack filled with full whisky bottles tied to his saddle. While on the trail, he met a Quilchena Native friend who demanded a drink from one of Coutlee's bottles. When Coutlee refused him, the man jumped behind him on the horse and stabbed him repeatedly in the back before running away. Some of Coutlee's cowboys brought him into the Merritt hospital where he was attended by Dr. J.J. Gillis. As he stitched up Coutlee's back, the doctor shook his head. If the knife had been an inch longer, it would have killed him. As it was, Coutlee was back at work within a few days.

Coutlee moved cattle for the last time in the fall of 1944 but he did not ride that winter. The following July, he was moved to St. Paul's Hospital in Vancouver for treatment for a cancerous growth on his neck. That fall, a friend visited him in St. Paul's and asked him when he was coming back to Douglas Lake. Coutlee replied, "Thursday." Sure enough, that Thursday Joe Coutlee's coffin was returned to his home in the Interior. He was buried in the little Native cemetery at Shulus, with the entire Nicola Valley in attendance.[8]

Jim Bonner

In the course of tending to cattle, accidents happened and sometimes it was hours before anyone could be found to bandage up a cut or set a bone. So cowboys had to learn to "grin and bear it" if they were in pain. However, Jim Bonner's experience went far beyond the grin-and-bear-it stage. Bonner worked for Dick Church on his Big Creek Ranch and was gathering up stray cattle in the fall of 1942 in the Hungry Valley, an isolated valley high up in the foothills of the Coast Range. Bonner was working with Jimmy Rosette, who was looking for Gang Ranch cattle in the remote area, when Bonner's horse slipped on a frost-covered side hill and fell on him. Bonner's leg was shattered between the knee and ankle but the only way out was on horseback. Rosette helped him back into the saddle and, with the broken leg not even splinted, the two men rode 12 miles down to Fosbery Meadow where there was a cabin. The cowboys spent the night at the cabin and Rosette managed to fashion a makeshift splint. Once again, Bonner was helped into the saddle for another 12-mile ride through swamp and Jack pine to Gus Piltz's Sky Ranch, situated at about 5,000 feet elevation. By now the pain must have been unbearable but Bonner, whitefaced and grim, kept silent. From the Sky Ranch, Bonner travelled in the back of Piltz's pickup truck over a rough road to the Church Ranch at Big Creek. But the ordeal was far from over. At Big Creek, Bonner was loaded into the back of a car, which proceeded toward Williams Lake. But the combination of rain and snow made the road almost impassable and the going was extremely slow. The 75-mile trip to Williams Lake took nine hours! After three incredibly painful days and nights, Bonner arrived at the hospital where his broken bones were set. Throughout the whole ordeal, he had kept quiet and refrained from complaining.[9]

Bill Arnold

In the late fall, ranchers who had cattle and horses would gather the cattle first and leave the horses to rustle for themselves. This usually took until about Christmas, after which the ranches with horses on the range would start bringing them in for the coldest part of the winter. The older, wiser horses would wander down to the lower country but many others preferred to take their chances in the high country. This was the worst time of year for cowboys. They would spend weeks on horseback in bitter January and February weather looking for stragglers. Often they would come upon a stallion with his harem of mares, or occasionally an old mare would have a small bunch of horses following her. The younger horses were the worst to bring in. They tended to separate from the bunch and, when finally located, were difficult to drive.

Bill Arnold was well known as a bronc rider, one of the toughest jobs on any ranch. One cold winter day, he was out hunting horses with Alex Bulman in the Stump Lake range, looking for straggler horses that would rather fend for themselves than return to the lower country to be fed by the ranchers. Finding these outlaw horses was a bit like tracking deer. Arnold and Bulman followed tracks in the snow to determine travel patterns and looked for fresh tracks that indicated that the horses had moved to a new feeding area. On this particular day, the cowboys were lucky and found the fresh tracks of four two-year-old horses. As soon as the two men got close, the horses went on the run. The men got behind them and began to work them in the direction of home, but something on the trail spooked them and they split into two groups. Bulman went after one pair and Arnold the other. Bulman managed to get his pair out of the timber and back to the home ranch before dark but there was no sign of Bill Arnold. All through the cold winter night, Bulman wondered where Arnold had gotten to but wasn't too worried. Arnold was an experienced hand and could look after himself. The next morning Bulman rode out to look for him. He had gone about three miles when he found Arnold riding slowly without the young horses. He related that, in his mad ride through the bush, his horse had run him into a sharp-pointed log that was sticking out. The log had hit Arnold in the ribs and knocked him to the ground. His saddle horse had taken off and Arnold was in no condition to walk, so he made a fire in a big dry log, huddled as close as he could to it through the night and waited for help to arrive. When daylight came, Arnold's horse returned to him and he managed to struggle back on to ride out, albeit in considerable pain. There was no question that Arnold had broken or cracked some ribs but he refused to see a doctor, preferring to lie down and lick his wounds. After about 10 days of being unable to move, he was back in the saddle again. Not bad for a 70-year-old man! [10]

Alex and Celina Kalelest

Alex Kalelest was a Shuswap Native who was born in 1885, a member of a small band that lived on the west side of the Fraser River. He had a small ranch on Gaspard Creek near the Gang Ranch's Home Ranch Valley. In 1940, he had a few cows that were so fat they could not be bred, so he put them in the Big Creek cattle drive that included cattle from the Blenkinsops, Bambricks and Wittes and rode with the much younger cowboys on the overland drive through Farwell canyon to the Williams Lake stockyards. It was not uncommon to have cowboys who were in their 50s on cattle drives. In fact, once cattle are settled into a drive, it is relatively easy work for a good horseman to keep them confined in a herd. Val Haynes, the famous South Okanagan cowboy, drove cattle on his

Douglas Lake Ranch cowboys. Native cowboys from the nearby Spahomin Reserve were an integral part of the Douglas Lake crews. *Historic O'Keefe Ranch photo*

87th birthday. Also along on that drive was Kalelest's daughter, Celina, and her young children who accompanied him with his camp outfit in a team and wagon. One night, Celina quietly gave birth to a baby without a doctor or midwife anywhere in the neighbourhood. The next morning, she was out gathering firewood as usual as the cattle drive continued.[11]

A Year at the Douglas Lake Ranch

On large ranches like Douglas Lake, cowboys spent most of their time in the saddle. Separate crews were hired for haying, irrigating and other work. Except for minor changes, the yearly cycle remained the same for decades as the cowboys moved from one job to another, and from one range to another, depending upon the season. Throughout British Columbia, the yearly cycle of moving cattle was similar, only varying depending upon climate and elevation.

In May, when the ice had disappeared off Douglas Lake where the ranch headquarters was located, preparations began for the spring exodus. Horses were run in from their winter range and the cowboys selected their "string" of strong young horses for summer work. A heavy freight wagon was backed into the lake to allow the wooden wheels and spokes to swell tight against the iron rims. The four horses chosen to pull the freight wagon were selected not for their looks but because they were too "rank" to ride and needed some time in harness to adjust their attitudes a bit. All the groceries, cooking utensils, fresh vegetables, eggs and beef were loaded into the wagon and covered with a tarp. Then the cowboys' bedrolls and duffle bags were thrown on top and the wagon was ready to roll. It was time for goodbyes. The horses would be harnessed up and attached to the wagon, which was backed up tight to a snubbing post and tied tight with a rope. Beneath the rope was a block of wood and, as the horses pulled and reared in harness, the teamster, Hank Loewen, would call out, "Turn 'em loose!" The rope was chopped, the horses leapt into action and the wagon careened out of the yard, the teamster gripping the reins and his brakeman pulling back hard on the brake lever. Behind the wagon were two cowboys at the head of 100 head of horses full of energy and oats. Following the herd were six or eight cowboys riding at an easy lope, and behind them were the mares and foals led by two cowboys. The mares had just been introduced to the stallion who would be their "companion" for the summer and excitement ran through the herd. It was officially spring at the Douglas Lake Ranch.[12] Most of the cowboys would not be back until November.

It was "turn out" time, when most of the cattle were driven to the various summer ranges in the higher elevations on the ranch. One crew would drive about 4,000 head of yearling steers and two- and three-year-old heifers with bulls toward the north end of the ranch so they could graze from the Salmon River west to Pennask Lake. Another 6,000 head, including cows with calves on them and stock for market, were driven south with Joe Coutlee in charge of them.

The dry cows and fat market steers were then driven across Quilchena Creek to the Wilson Springs area where they would continue to fatten up. From there, it was a relatively short drive to the railhead at Nicola. The Wilson Springs cow camp consisted of a single log cookshack and a large corral for horses. The springs provided cool water to the cookshack through a steel pipe that had been driven into the hillside. For accommodation, the cowboys would pitch a couple of tents on the flat area above the cookshack. The tents used at Douglas Lake were 8 feet by 12 feet, with lumber floors and 4-foot-high walls to which the tent was attached.

From Wilson Springs, the cattle were driven into the railway stockyards at Nicola to be loaded into cattle cars. The big ranches in the area—including the Douglas Lake, the Quilchena Cattle Company, Nicola Stock Farms and the Whiteford Ranch—all brought their cattle to market through the Nicola stockyards. The herds of cattle were driven in and then cut out and weighed. The scales were owned by the Douglas Lake Ranch and the stockyards were owned by the CPR. The brand inspector, Jimmy Batten, weighed the cattle and checked their brands before they were driven right into the cattle cars by cowboys on horseback. Sometimes a cowboy would have to ride right into the chute to push a reluctant steer into the cattle car and then back his horse out. A man was stationed to pull the sliding platform back from the train and slide the boxcar door shut. One car could hold 23 two-year-old steers but fewer than 20 big cows.

Most cowboys spent the summer in one cow camp or another, or in a series of cow camps. When the grass in one area had been grazed down, the crew and camp would move to another cow camp. The crews were mostly Native cowboys. All their belongings, plus groceries, tents, stove and cooking

Crew and cook at Chilco Ranch. Women who cooked for the cowboys on the remote corners of the big ranches had to be strong and resourceful. *Museum of the Cariboo Chilcotin, Williams Lake photo*

utensils, would be piled into a heavy wagon and a four-horse team would pull the wagon over rough terrain to the next location. At the north end of the Douglas Lake Ranch, the cowboys would start out at the old McDonald place near the Norfolk Ranch that had been acquired by Douglas Lake in 1921. This camp had log cabins and big barns that could be used by the crew. From there, the camp moved on to Jenny's Flats, where the camp was all tents, and then the next site would be at the head of Chapperon Lake, where there was an old granary that could be used as a cookhouse. In late summer, the cattle were moved to the Lewis corrals, at a higher elevation, where the cook and cowboys would live in tents until fall roundup. Two tents were combined in a "T" shape, one end being the cook tent and the other the dining room. Native women from the Spahomin Reserve usually did the cooking and the cookstove would be right inside the tent.

The cow camp at the south end of the Douglas Lake Ranch was the Raspberry Camp at Minnie Lake. It had a bunkhouse with enough beds for 16 cowboys. The "facilities" consisted of an outhouse. To wash their clothes, the cowboys would hang them by a rope in the creek, let the running water do the rest and then throw the "clean" clothes over a fence to dry.

Breakfast in the summer months was at 3:00 a.m., the cooks and wranglers having already been up for an hour. No one had an alarm clock; they just woke up. If they didn't, the cow boss, usually Joe Coutlee at the Raspberry Camp, would wake them up with his booming voice or his foot. Two cowboys normally took a turn at wrangling in the early morning. There would be two "stake horses" in the corral that would be used for bringing in the other horses. As soon as the cowboy's foot hit the stirrup, the stake horse would be off at a gallop, knowing exactly what it was supposed to do. The horses that had been out all night had bells on them so they could be located in the dark. As soon as the wranglers got to where they expected to find the horses, they would start to holler and bells would start ringing as the horses came in. The wranglers would ride behind the bells to pick up stragglers and push the herd into the corral where they could be roped and saddled. Each cowboy roped his horse with a flashlight in one hand and a rope in the other, and then saddled up in the dark. Four or five cowboys would work in the corral at one time and saddle up, but not without receiving a few well-placed kicks from the sleepy horses. By the time they were finished, the cooks had breakfast ready. Breakfast during the Second World War was usually steak, potatoes and eggs as it was impossible to get bacon, all of the available supply having gone overseas. The ranch supplied fresh beef for the camp, usually prime yearling, so the cowboys could always enjoy excellent beef. The cooks would also have bread that had been baked the day before and plenty of coffee to wash down the food. Most cowboys drank their coffee from the saucer, where it would cool quicker. Then they were off for the day, not to return until mid-afternoon or later. They had to get to the cattle when the cows and calves were still "mothered up," before daylight.

The cow boss was in charge at cow camp. He decided where to move the cattle and assigned a task to every cowboy. He would send cowboys in each direction and tell them where to bring the cattle. The cowboys would be expected to keep an eye on the cattle to make sure they were on the best grass and to keep the bulls from bunching up in one place. This was to ensure that the bulls spread out enough to breed all the cows and to keep the bulls from fighting. The cowboys also did a lot of doctoring on the cattle. Pink eye and foot rot were the most common problems. Two riders would work together so that one could rope the head and the other the back legs to bring the animal down. The cure for pink eye involved pouring a solution in the cow's eyes. To treat foot rot, they would run a rope between the animal's toes to clean them and then spray on a foot rot preparation. The cowboys would not take a lunch with them and were hungry before they got back to cow camp.

Left to right: Alkali Lake cowboys Melvin Mayfield on Doc, Bill Twan on Cannon Ball and Hermie Maurice on Cricket. *Museum of the Cariboo Chilcotin, Williams Lake photo*

But when they arrived, two, three or four at a time, they would be greeted by a meal of more fresh beef—roasted, boiled or stewed—with dumplings. But first they had to look after their horses and make sure they were turned out to pasture with the rest of the *remuda*. Then they would make sure that, if they needed a "wrangle horse" for morning, it was in the corral.

The ranch horses in the 1940s were Morgan crosses and not noted for their gentle nature. For the summer, cowboys usually had 8 or 10 horses in their string so that as many horses as possible could be ridden to "get the kinks out." Bill Copeland, who worked for the ranch at the time recalled, "Douglas Lake had some really bad horses at the time and I was a kind of bronc rider, so I got the bad ones. I had to top them off in the morning and some of them at lunchtime. They were just starting to get the Morgan cross horses at Douglas Lake. Terrible things! They couldn't turn around in forty acres of land, and they would fall over every stump in the country."[13] Generally, the cow boss would tell each cowboy which horse to ride for the day but, if the cowboy had his own string already, he would ride each one in turn, providing they came in with the wrangle herd.

This daily routine continued at the cow camps through the summer and into the fall until it was time to round up cattle and drive them to the winter feeding areas. In late fall, the cattle were rounded up from the high country. Once again, Joe Coutlee would be in charge of the roundup. Each rider was given three big saddle horses, referred to as "long circle horses." Unlike the Morgan cross horses used through the summer months, these big-boned horses were usually a mix of thoroughbred and native cayuse, with a trace of Clydesdale. They could travel at a fast trot for great distances and never seemed to tire. In short, even though they weren't pretty, they were just the horses for a long day's ride.

Once the cattle were gathered, calves were separated from their mothers for weaning and moved to different places on the ranch where they would be fed hay for the winter. Cattle, for the most part, will move down out of the hills when the colder weather comes. But there would always be a few stragglers that would linger in some swamp meadow until they ran out of feed. When this happened, they would face starvation unless they were found, so a few of the cowboys would have to spend the first part of winter looking for stray cattle. Most of the cowboys, however, were laid off for the winter and went into town or back to their reserves until spring.

About 1,200 head of cattle were driven down to Westwold where Robert Clemitson was contracted to feed them. Another 2,500 head were fed at the Norfolk Ranch, the Chapperon Lake Ranch fed about 3,000 head and the Home Ranch another 5,000 to 6,000 head. The ideal feeding number was about 500 head in one bunch. Any more than this number and the weaker cattle would not get enough to eat because of competition from the stronger, more aggressive cattle that wanted more than their share, so the ranch hands built long fences and broke the herd into bunches of 500 to 600 head. This method proved to be a more efficient way of using the hay and it proved to be easier on the cows. A teamster would drive a team of horses and two helpers would load the loose hay on a rack to spread out for the cattle. The haystacks were fenced and the hay was forked out in a long line so that all the cattle could get at it. It was generally reckoned that it would take a ton of hay per 100 head of stock per day to keep the cattle healthy. Once the feed grounds grew too dirty, the cattle were moved to another spot to feed.

Wherever large stacks of hay were being fed to the cattle, at least one cowboy was on hand through the winter to ride through the herd to check for sick cattle and to help move cattle from one feed ground to another. The cowboys would also chop through the ice to keep the water holes open and keep an eye out for predators. Bears were always a problem, especially during calving. Both grizzly and black bears were common at Douglas Lake but the black bears were actually more destructive. Grizzlies would kill an animal and feed on it until all the meat was gone but a black bear could get into the habit of killing a calf just for a meal. Black bears would also return to kill

Winter cattle drive in the Chilcotin. During the winter months, cattle were fed from a haystack until it was exhausted and then were driven to the next haystack in a nearby meadow.
Museum of the Cariboo Chilcotin, Williams Lake photo

Hauling hay for winter feed on Clarke Ranch, north of Williams Lake. Once the snow got deeper, a sleigh had to be used to haul hay. *Museum of the Cariboo Chilcotin, Williams Lake photo*

from the herd many times and could become quite aggressive toward any person who came into their territory. Once a black bear developed a taste for calves, it would do a lot of damage until it was removed, whereas grizzlies would kill once and move on. During the winter months, cougars would also take a few yearlings. At the Douglas Lake Ranch, Charlie Shuttleworth, the predator hunter, was kept busy hunting the bears and occasional cougars that preyed on stock. The daily routine of feeding cattle went on through the dark days of winter until spring appeared again and the yearly cycle began anew.

Ranchers Take On the Market

During the early 1940s, the grip of the packing houses on the ranching industry continued to tighten. The Wartime Prices and Trade Board set a low ceiling price for the sale of cattle and the packers once again held the advantage. Ranchers throughout the province decided it was time to do something about the packers' stranglehold on an industry that was worth $25 million and had annual livestock sales averaging $5 million. They felt that they should be strong enough to deal with the packing houses. The obvious answer was for the ranchers to band together and market their cattle directly to the meat packers. But, among the fiercely independent ranchers, the thought of organizing into co-operatives was alien to their thinking. As Harry Marriott recalled:

> It has bothered me considerably as to why the ranchers and farmers have always been so backward and indifferent toward organization of any kind on a co-operative, or union, or association basis. So many of them would give lip service, but when it came to the actual stand together, final jump, they shied around it, like a cold-shouldered horse. I have often wondered if many of our ranchers are defeatists at heart, having been jammed around by the packers and middlemen, commission men and so on, for so long and so successfully, that they get an attitude that they are licked before they start. Every business I know of has some form of protective association except these ranchers and farmers who have only played around with the fringes of collective organization.[14]

But just as the cattlemen had dealt with the lowest prices in memory through the 1930s, so too they began to look for another way of selling other than through cattle buyers, from whom they were obliged to take whatever they were offered after having driven their cattle to a central location.

George Mayfield of the 141 Mile Ranch had read extensively on marketing principles and practices and was determined to change the *status quo*. He began renting pastures and offering one cent a pound over the price the packers were offering at Williams Lake. Ranchers in the area would drive their cattle to Mayfield's holding area rather than to the stockyards in Williams Lake. From there, Mayfield would sell directly to the meat packers, who were willing to give him a good price because of the volume of cattle he controlled. When the cattle buyers, who had always insisted that they were offering the best price possible, saw that their supply of cattle was starting to dwindle they would offer an additional quarter cent a pound to the ranchers. Mayfield would then promptly raise his price by a quarter cent. Despite several rounds of price raises, the ranchers noticed that Mayfield still sold all the cattle that had been brought to him at a profit. It was obvious that the ranchers had not been receiving the true value of their stock. So, in 1940, the Cariboo Cattlemen's Association set up the Cariboo Marketing Agency with George Mayfield as the fieldman, a middleman between the rancher and buyer. By 1945, 97 percent of all the cattle shipped between 100 Mile House and Williams Lake were being sold through the marketing agency and morale among ranchers was noticeably improved.

Ranchers in the southern Interior had an advantage in marketing cattle because they did not have extremely long drives to bring their cattle to buying

Auction pen in the Williams Lake stockyards. By the mid-1940s, the Cariboo Marketing Agency that had been set up by the Cariboo Cattlemen's Association was selling most of the cattle at Williams Lake.
Museum of the Cariboo Chilcotin, Williams Lake photo

points. The Kettle Valley Railway, operated by the CPR after 1931, wound its way through the Boundary, South Okanagan and Princeton areas, providing direct access to the Vancouver markets. Beyond that though, the situation was much the same as it was in the Cariboo–Chilcotin. One buyer would come to the ranches and make an offer, followed a few days later by another buyer. No competitive bidding took place at the ranch level. If a rancher was in a gambling mood, he could ship his cattle directly to Vancouver and take his chances at the stockyards there. Things came to a head when Vern Fetterly and Angus Smith, two South Okanagan ranchers, sent their cattle by rail to Vancouver for sale. They were loaded on cattle cars at Okanagan Falls and never heard of again. Neither the railway nor the Vancouver stockyards would take any responsibility for the loss and the ranchers had no success in obtaining any retribution.

In 1942, ranchers from the southern Interior gathered under a tree at the Kettle Valley Railway stockyards in Okanagan Falls to establish the Southern Interior Stockmen's Association and elect a board of directors to represent the area from Rock Creek to the Similkameen Valley. Not surprisingly, Vern

Fetterly, whose cattle had gone "missing in action" on the way to Vancouver, was one of the directors. The organization needed its own stockyards to be able to market cattle effectively and approached the CPR for assistance. The railway donated railroad ties for posts and bridge timbers to build a sale yard at Okanagan Falls. Several work bees were held to cut the timbers into two-by-six boards and to construct the yards. From then on, regular sales were conducted and the volume of cattle sold through this outlet continued to grow.

The success of the Cariboo Marketing Agency and the Southern Interior Stockmen's Association indicated that there was a need for similar organizations in the Kamloops and Nicola areas. Things came to a head in 1943 when the Vancouver stockyards, which had been operated by the BC Livestock Exchange, were offered for sale by the owners who had fallen into arrears in their payments. Fortunately, the provincial minister of trade and commerce at the time, who was responsible for foreclosing on the mortgage, was Ernie Carson, a rancher. He encouraged his brother, Bob Carson, to talk to the ranchers in the Kamloops and Nicola Valley areas about possibly purchasing the stockyards. At first, the large ranches proposed that a limited company be formed to sell shares in the yards, but most ranchers opposed this idea, believing that the large ranches would control the company to their own advantage. The discussions continued. At a meeting in the Plaza Hotel in Kamloops that summer, Bill McLeod, a rancher from Westwold, proposed the establishment of a co-operative selling agency on the basis of "one man, one vote." To put his money where his mouth was, he pledged $100. This gesture had an impact on the ranchers who were desperate to get something happening. As Alex Bulman said at the time, "Bill McLeod was a man who did not have too many one hundred dollar bills to throw around." [15] So the motion was seconded, discussed and passed and the BC Livestock Producers Co-operative Association (BCLPCA) was formed. The organization of all the cattlemen in the province was finally realized. Brian Chance, the manager of the Douglas Lake Ranch, was elected president and Lord Martin Cecil, the president of the Cariboo Cattlemen's Association, was vice-president.

The availability of the Vancouver stockyards seemed like the perfect opportunity for the fledgling BCLPCA but there was competition for their purchase from a group of livestock dealers, most of whom did not have a good reputation among the ranchers. The BCLPCA therefore began spreading the word among the ranchers and asking for memberships. Within a few weeks, the organization had raised $5,000 but that was far short of the required $25,000. Once again, Ernie Carson, who was then acting minister of agriculture, went into action. He persuaded the provincial government to put up the extra money and take out a mortgage on the stockyards. It seemed that the ranchers of the province were finally in the marketing business.

Things did not proceed smoothly for the new organization. Although the loan from the government was paid off within a few years, the money raised from commissions on sales was barely enough to cover the operating costs. This left little to no capital money for improvements to the stockyards. There were also territorial concerns over those men working in the field, and conflicts between those selling their cattle in the field and those selling them at auction. There seemed to be little consistency between the standards and prices offered in the field and those at the auction yards. These problems were solved by establishing more rigid boundaries for fieldmen and protocols for the sale of cattle. The main problem, however, was the need for repairs to the Vancouver stockyards. Lord Martin Cecil, who was president of the Cariboo Cattlemen's Association, offered to lend $2,000 of the association's money to help with repairs and the necessary maintenance was completed. Other major concerns were slow payments for the cattle and conflicting sale dates. But, despite the ongoing problems, the organization continued to provide rancher-owned and rancher-operated services and today operates four stockyards in Williams Lake, Kamloops, Okanagan Falls and Vanderhoof.

Nature Strikes Again

Wood Ticks

In the early 1930s, cowboys at the Douglas Lake Ranch noticed that about 100 steers in a herd of 900 seemed to be getting paralyzed. Eric Hearle, the entomologist at the Livestock Insect Laboratory in Kamloops, was asked to take a look at them and immediately spotted the problem. The steers were infested with Rocky Mountain wood ticks, hosting up to 150 ticks on the backs of their heads and between their shoulders. This was the first major outbreak of tick paralysis in cattle in the province.

The Rocky Mountain wood tick is a bloodsucking parasite that lives on animals and humans. Although many people believe that these wood ticks are only found in heavily wooded country, the greatest concentrations are usually found in areas such as river valleys, where soil temperature and moisture conditions favour their development. In their first year of a two- to four-year life cycle, they are usually found on mice, chipmunks, squirrels and other rodents. As adults, they are usually found on dogs, sheep, goats, cattle, deer and humans. In cattle they crawl up onto the withers and head of the animal where they fasten on and begin feeding. They inject a toxin into the animal that causes paralysis and sometimes death. They are also a carrier of the organism that causes Rocky Mountain spotted fever.

Eliminating this pest over large areas was not feasible. Clearing areas of brush, weeds and other low vegetation helped to control the pest, and controlling rodents and other small host animals also helped.

But prevention was the first measure to take. During April and May, cattle had to be kept off ranges that were known to have ticks: open rocky bunchgrass areas with southern exposure. If ticks were discovered, the cattle had to be removed as soon as possible. Treating cattle for wood ticks was relatively simple once they were detected. They could usually be scraped off with curry combs or even bare hands; the more stubborn ticks could be removed by applying kerosene or a mixture of linseed oil and pine tar. A single wood tick can paralyze a human, so the cowboys had to be extremely careful when dealing with them. Initially, wood ticks caused heavy losses to cattle in the Nicola Valley but once these practices were in place the problems diminished significantly.

Grasshoppers

In 1943, the grasshoppers came back. The grasshopper plagues of the 1930s had been from the clear-winged, or roadside, grasshopper (*Camnula pellucida*) whose females lay their eggs in large beds. This made their control easier and the Grasshopper Control Committee was able to spray arsenic on the beds. But this time there were more red-legged grasshoppers (*Melanoplus femurrubrum*). This type does not lay its eggs in communal beds, making it far more difficult to control. The situation was worsened because the Second World War made insecticides difficult to obtain and limited the number of men and trucks available to spray. Laurie Graham, who was supervising the control of grasshoppers at the Douglas Lake Ranch Dry Farm, knew the cyclical nature of grasshopper infestations and predicted that the following year would be worse. He was right. One of the worst grasshopper outbreaks in the province's history descended on the Nicola Valley in 1944. Even though ranchers had been preparing for the outbreak with insecticides and trucks ready to go, the plague soon got out of control. Brian Chance, manager of the Douglas Lake Ranch wrote, "The grasshoppers are just about in command here now, and in places are shearing the range and in some cases the hay meadows, particularly the second crop, as effectively as a scythe." [16] Entire ranges were clipped clean and trees lost all their leaves in a single day. A layer of dead grasshoppers covered the surface of every pond, stream and lake, and horses balked at riding into the stream of grasshoppers hitting them in the face. Roads were covered with an oily pulp of dead grasshoppers and their dead bodies greased the railway tracks, making it difficult for trains to stop. By the end of the year, the Nicola Grasshopper Control Committee had spent $17,000, mostly on insecticides, and the grasshoppers were on the decline again.

Warble Flies

The adult warble fly has a black, hairy body marked with yellow to orange stripes and resembles a small bumblebee. Warble flies are active in the spring and early summer, when the females lay their eggs. They can be so thick that they drive cattle into a frenzy as they chase them through the bush looking for a host to lay their eggs on. A favourite location is the hair on the legs, belly and flanks of cattle. The egg-laying activities of warble flies drive cattle into running or gadding, which interferes with normal grazing, reduces milk flow and sometimes causes injuries. The tiny, barely visible eggs hatch in two to seven days and the larvae (grubs) burrow through the skin and migrate through the body until they reach the animal's back, where they produce the characteristic lumps, or warbles. It takes seven to nine months for them to migrate to the animal's back where each warble has a breathing hole made by the grub and these openings sometimes lead to infection. When moving through an animal's body, the grubs may injure its esophagus and affect its ability to eat, resulting in loss of weight, or they may injure its spinal cord, causing paralysis. Infected animals have lower market values because of the carcass trimming required and because they leave a hole in the hide, making it unfit for leather. Ranchers around Okanagan Falls, where warble flies are common, would bring their animals together every spring and spray their cattle with the insecticide Rotenone. The chemical was more successful when it was rubbed on with a brush so cattle would be run through a chute to be treated. Cowboys would use a wooden-handled scrub brush that they dipped into a pail and rubbed on the cattle, making sure that the hair was penetrated. It took two or three days to spray for every ranch in the area.

Poisonous Plants

Northwest of Kamloops lie the sweeping grasslands, cool, dry forests and small lakes of the Lac du Bois area. The area is unique in that, as the land rises north and westward from the hot, dry Thompson valleys, it passes through three grassland communities. Nowhere else in western North America will you find these grassland communities in such close proximity to each other. Spring comes early to the lower hot, dry slopes with plants responding to the short, moist season. In contrast, the upper grasslands of bluebunch wheatgrass are not in full bloom until early June when brilliant yellow sunflowers wash the hillsides. Adding to the beauty of this area are the numerous varieties of flowering plants. The area seems like a perfect location for grazing cattle but one of these flowering plants makes the area deadly to cattle. Blue larkspur, also known as wild delphinium, is pleasing to the eye but is extremely poisonous, especially in June when it is in its most luxurious growth. Alex Bulman described the disastrous effect it had on cattle. "I will not soon forget the sight of 12 fat, two-year-old steers dead and bloated, their four legs pointed toward the sky. They had evidently taken on a big fill of larkspur and then headed for water. Some died on the edge of the lake, while others were lying at various distances along the trail."[17] The obvious answer was to know your range and keep the cattle out of the affected area during the deadly season of June.

Canadian milk vetch is another problem plant. It is found in timbered areas and remains green after other grasses have died. This makes it attractive to cattle but in cool, wet weather it can cause general weakness and even partial paralysis. If the cattle are not quickly moved onto different pasture where they can eat nutritious grasses they will die. Horses can also be affected by milk vetch. Their breathing becomes laboured, causing a loud snoring sound as the animal struggles to get enough air into its lungs. When a horse becomes stressed by the difficulty, it can often fall over as though in a fit. Usually this reaction is a passing problem and the horse quickly recovers and is able to travel again. Young animals usually recover but, in older animals, eating milk vetch can be fatal.

Purebred Cattle

In the late 1880s and early 1890s, the introduction of purebred cattle into the previously mixed-breed herds initiated a significant change in the industry. Although some cattlemen had imported purebred Durham Shorthorn bulls to the Interior in the 1870s, most did not consider breed improvement to be of any significant value. By the 1880s, the Shorthorn-Spanish cross cows that had originally been driven into British Columbia from Oregon were bred to Hereford bulls. The resulting cattle could withstand severe winters and produce excellent beef. More and more white-faced Herefords appeared, but Durham Shorthorns (mostly a roan colour) predominated, with a few

Aberdeen Angus or Galloways in the mix. Polled Angus were also popular because of their adaptability to the hot, dry climate and their lack of horns, which made shipping by rail safer. As time went on, ranchers increasingly saw the Hereford as the best type of cattle for British Columbia conditions.

By the mid-1930s and early 1940s, more and more ranchers were seeing that using purebred Hereford bulls was a way of ensuring consistency and rapid weight gain. Ranchers like Vern Ellison, who owned the V-V Ranch in the central Okanagan, and Victor Spencer, at the Earlscourt ranch near Lytton, operated ranches that were solely for the development of purebred Hereford bulls. Ellison's Kalwood stock took their name from his ranch's location in

Prize bull Kalwood Domino, from the V-V Ranch, owned by Vern Ellison. Ellison's Kalwood stock took their names from his ranch's location in the orchard country between Kalamalka and Wood lakes in the Okanagan Valley. *Museum of the Cariboo Chilcotin, Williams Lake*

the orchard country between Kalamalka and Wood Lakes where Ellison claimed, "Apples and Herefords Help Each Other to Perfection." Ellison actually fed apple pulp from juicing to his Herefords as winter silage. Under the care of Ellison's herdsman, Harold Somerset, Kalwood Herefords won championships all across BC and at the Toronto Royal Winter Fair. Both Kalwood and Earlscourt bulls could be found on ranches across the province and the Prairies.

Gung Loy Jim was the son of a storekeeper, Kam Kee, a second-generation Chinese who owned and operated the Jim Man Lee store in Mount Olie, later called Little Fort. In 1938, he started a fishing camp at Taweel Lake, but because Chinese were not allowed to lease Crown land, he had to have a partner, Tom Humble, to take out the lease. The camp was

Gung Loy Jim fulfilled his dream of raising purebred Herefords on land near Little Fort. His Little Fort Herefords were among the finest cattle in the province. *Silver Cartwright photo*

so successful, attracting well-heeled people from all over the world, that he managed to fulfill his dream of raising purebred Herefords on land near Little Fort. Beginning in 1943 with six cows, he built up his herd of Little Fort Herefords. He continued improving the quality of his Herefords by the extensive use of artificial insemination and purchasing select cattle from the top herds in Canada. His bulls were his pride and joy and won several grand championships at the Kamloops Provincial Bull Sale. Jim was an astute judge of Hereford conformation and, when ranchers were looking for large-framed, fast-growing cattle to compete with the exotic breeds in the early 1970s, he was recognized as one of the foremost breeders in the country with cattle that had the genetic characteristics that ranchers were looking for. As he grew older, he spent his time working on the ranch and driving his tractor to oversee his beloved Herefords. Jim's eyesight eventually began to fade and his sons suggested that he stop driving the tractor because he couldn't see too well. He replied, "Hell, I know my way around the farm well enough to drive by the Braille method." His sons agreed that this was probably true only if you were not particularly concerned about gates and fences. In 1993, Gung Loy Jim was honoured at the Kamloops Bull Sale for his 50 years of membership in the Canadian Hereford Association. That year he entered four bulls in the sale, took three first-place ribbons and one second, and received Junior Champion, Junior Reserve Champion, Senior Champion and Grand Reserve Champion honours. As well, his bulls won Best Pair and Best Group of Four. His sons continue to operate Little Fort Herefords as a commercial family ranch.

Returning Soldiers

During the war years, many Canadian soldiers had been trained in British Columbia at Camp Vernon, Gordon Head, Chilliwack, Esquimalt, Courtenay, Nanaimo and Vancouver. Others had served alongside British Columbians who waxed lyrical about their province. So it was not surprising that, after the war, thousands of returning soldiers, airmen and sailors came to British Columbia to resettle.

At the close of the Second World War, a grateful country looked for ways of assisting the returning soldiers in becoming re-established in Canada. There was a Canadian tradition dating from the 17th century of settling ex-soldiers on the land,[18] and the 1919 Soldier Settlement Act had provided returning First World War veterans who wished to farm or ranch with loans to purchase land, stock and equipment. Over 25,000 men took advantage of the scheme but the land that was available at the time was on the fringes of suitable land for farming or ranching. Many veterans had to abandon their farms between the wars because of heavy debts and adverse farming conditions. Determined not to see a repeat of this occurrence, the government passed the Veterans' Land Act (VLA) in July 1942. The VLA, designed to overcome some of the problems inherent to the 1919 plan, actively purchased land in the British Columbia Interior that was suitable for farming and ranching so that returning veterans could be given a choice of where to settle. With only a small down payment, ex-servicemen could purchase land with the help of a government loan and additional funds were available for buying livestock and equipment. Repayment terms allowed settlers time to re-establish themselves without incurring heavy financial obligations.

Tim Bayliffe, whose grandfather Hugh had been a mud pup in the Chilcotin in the 1880s, was one of the ex-servicemen who benefitted. He had served in the Canadian Navy during the war, doing anti-piracy peace patrol in the South China Sea. In 1946, he returned to the Chilcotin and purchased the Christy Ranch through the VLA. He was allowed to borrow up to $5,000 at 5 percent interest toward the $15,000 cost of purchasing the ranch. At the time, the amount seemed astronomical but hard work and the buoyant postwar market soon helped him pay off the loan.

The VLA purchased land throughout the Interior during the war in anticipation of the demand for land from the returning servicemen and with the intention of making good farms and ranches available. One of the areas picked was on the benchland around K Mountain near Cawston in the Similkameen Valley. Although the land was excellent orchard land with irrigation available, the veterans who purchased land in this location grew hay to supplement their income until their orchards reached productive levels. Hal Tweddle, who ranched in the area, saw an opportunity and started custom baling. He soon had 29 customers during haying season. Alice Tweddle, Hal's wife and partner (in more ways than one), explained her involvement: "We ran that baler 24 hours a day if there was no dew, because everyone wanted hay done at the same time. I could fix a motor, oil and grease those big balers, I even drove tractors to pull them! . . . The boys helped bail until 12:00 p.m. at night [sic], and we sent them to school the next day! The knotters were very complicated but I could do them, grease balers, and go looking for Hal in the night through orchards, and take him food and gas." [19]

The VLA also purchased large tracts of land in the Westwold area during the war years. While the war was going on, the land was rented out; at the end of the war, it was made available for veterans. One of them was Stewart Forde, who had been born and raised at François Lake in northern BC. After serving in the army through the war, he married and began to look for land, checking all the newspapers at the library. In the *Winnipeg Free Press*, he noticed land near Westwold advertised and thought he'd check it out. He and his wife, Margaret, headed off in their only vehicle, a two-ton truck. As they navigated the narrow, winding road they came around one tight corner with one of their dual back wheels hanging over the edge! They swore right there and then that they would never live in a place like that. Then they turned another corner and saw a beautiful wooded property nestled in the trees beside the meadows around Westwold. They were sold. They purchased the land through a VLA loan and never looked back.

John McLeod was another serviceman who purchased land in the Westwold area. He had been brought up in nearby Barnhartvale and moved to Westwold in 1933. McLeod became a cowboy when a local veterinarian gave him a cow. The cow was cross-eyed but certainly not handicapped in any other way and showed it by escaping when the family moved from Barnhartvale to Westwold. McLeod hopped on his saddle horse, his first, and tracked the animal down, thus beginning his career as a cattleman. McLeod signed on with the Royal Canadian Air Force in 1940 and served overseas for the duration of the war. When he returned home in 1945, he purchased two pieces of land near Westwold, totalling 330 acres, through the VLA. He worked for three years as a cowboy in the area to pay off the land and then purchased 20 head of cattle. He married Isobel Wood in 1947 and the two raised livestock, vegetables and crops of alfalfa and oats on their property. They retired in 1984.

Joe Pringle was another local boy who took advantage of VLA land in the Westwold area to get started. He joined the army in 1942 and, after basic training at Camp Vernon, went to Fort Benning in the United States to train as a paratrooper. On D-Day, he parachuted into France with the 6th Airborne Division and fought through Belgium and the Netherlands. He participated in the Battle of the Rhine and parachuted into the Rhine Crossing, eventually ending up in Wismar on the Baltic coast. After VE Day, his battalion returned home, only to be slated to go on to the Pacific. But he never made it to the Pacific as the dropping of the atomic bomb put an end to both the war and Pringle's career as a paratrooper. He returned to Westwold and purchased land through the VLA in 1946. He farmed, logged and ran a fishing camp for the next 26 years.

War Brides

There were a large number of small VLA holdings in the Westwold area and many of the returning servicemen who settled there brought back brides from Britain. For most of the brides, the transition from their comfortable homes in Britain to the Canadian wilderness was both difficult and frightening. Cecily Becker (née Joynson), who left the north of England to join her husband, Fred, was not impressed when she saw her new home on VLA land near Westwold. The kitchen was a lean-to roofed with rusted corrugated tin and tacked on to the back of the house. The water system consisted of a wooden culvert that ran from the well across the front yard and into a hole in the side of the house. And the "convenience" was down a sloping narrow path from the kitchen. Despite the incredible adjustments she had to make, Cecily persevered, as did hundreds like her all over Canada. In later years, she would reminisce that, "It is now fifty years since World War II. There aren't many veterans still farming. The Veterans Land Act must be a part of Canadian history, but I remember my dear Cockney friend Margaret coming out to marry her Dave. You could tell he was a Welshman—you'd hear him singing in the morning when he started his chores. I remember too Dot Watson. I was so impressed by the way she helped Hunter at lambing time." [20]

There were many other Westwold war brides, including one from Wales, one from Scotland and three from England. When a war bride arrived in the community, the Women's Auxiliary of St. Luke's Church would invite her to a surprise welcoming shower. The whole community reached out to embrace the war brides in their new homes, but no one was more welcoming than

Margaret Pearse. She had come from Scotland at the turn of the century but retained her "old country" ways to the end. Her strong black tea, raspberry vinegar and gingersnaps were an institution in the community. Children were always welcome in her home and she always had paints and crayons to keep them amused while the ladies had tea. But her heart was especially open to the war brides, and she would ride her bicycle to visit them regularly to offer words of encouragement and consolation. For the brides, far from home, she was like a mother, eager to listen and advise and it is safe to say that many of them would have struggled were it not for Mrs. Pearse.

Chapter Five

A New Era Dawns

With a cloud of dust, the herd of 300 head of cattle descended the hill to the Fraser River. Half a dozen cowboys on horseback, easily controlling the herd, emerged through the dust. They had begun the drive with 200 head of unwilling cattle and had added another 100 at Chezacut on the way. By now, they had been on the trail for the better part of two months and the cattle were weary and used to the routine. The famous Chimney Creek suspension bridge, completed in 1904, lay ahead. It was the final hurdle before the stockyards of Williams Lake. The wooden-decked bridge had been improved with steel towers in 1912 and re-decked several times. Early in its life, ranchers had found that it had a decided tendency to swing if too many cattle were on it at one time, so they had set up fenced pastures at either end of the bridge to hold the cattle as they were driven across 10 at a time. All summer long, cattle drives had been using the holding pastures on the western side to contain their cattle before pushing them across the bottleneck to the holding pasture on the eastern side. Ten head of cattle at a time meant 30 trips back and forth across the bridge, and it took the cowboys all day to complete the crossing. But the next day they would reach Williams Lake, the end of the drive.

Late the next day, the weary cattle and cowboys arrived at the Williams Lake stockyards. The grizzled trail boss, who had been in charge of the drive from the start, oversaw the final arrangements before he and his boys could turn around and ride back home. As he was doing this, he heard the roar of a large truck. He watched with interest as the transport truck pulled in to the stockyards and began unloading cattle. The trail boss walked up to the driver and asked, "Where are you bringing these cattle from?" The driver replied,

Louis Louis and Tierney O'Keefe branding at the O'Keefe Ranch near Vernon. *Historic O'Keefe Ranch photo*

Cattle stringing down the trail to the Chimney Creek bridge. Because the bridge had a tendency to sway, cattle were driven across 10 at a time. *Museum of the Cariboo Chilcotin, Williams Lake photo*

"Tatla Lake, about 250 miles from here." "When did you start?" asked the trail boss. The driver replied, "This morning." The trail boss shook his head and mumbled, "Things are changing in the cattle business."

Things were changing indeed. The 1950s brought significant changes to many aspects of the cattle industry in the British Columbia Interior. The postwar boom saw incredible growth in the industry as well as major changes in the way cattle were shipped and marketed. According to the British Columbia Beef Cattle Growers' Association, in 1948 there were 49,300 head of beef cattle in the Cariboo-Chilcotin-Lillooet districts and 48,700 head in the Thompson–Nicola and Princeton districts. Another 27,400 head could be found in the Okanagan and Boundary areas, making a total of over 125,000 head of cattle in the British Columbia Interior. By 1960, the number of cattle

Hereford bull at the O'Keefe Ranch near Vernon. By the 1950s, two-thirds of all cattle in British Columbia were Herefords. *Historic O'Keefe Ranch photo*

had increased by one-third to over 167,000 head of cattle. The 1950s were a time of unprecedented growth and change in the cattle industry.

The dominant breed was Hereford and fully two-thirds of all beef cattle were of this breed. The others were pure- or cross-bred Shorthorns, the general feeling being that the Shorthorn cows provided better milk and faster weight gain for calves. There were also scattered herds of Aberdeen Angus. Government regulations required that any bulls placed on Crown land had to be registered purebred animals and that there should be no fewer than 1 bull for every 30 head of cows in community breeding pastures. As a result, it is safe to say that, by the 1950s, almost all the bulls in the ranching area were purebred. These bulls would have been purchased at the Kamloops and Williams Lake annual bull sales, with a few imported from Alberta. Since the cost of purebred bulls was generally quite high, smaller ranchers would often buy bulls that had been passed on from large herds at a reduced price.

New Owners

Many of the ranches of British Columbia changed hands in the 1950s and, more often than not, the new owners were American. This was the result of a combination of factors. The generation of ranch owners who had purchased in the 1920s and 1930s were getting on in age and were also feeling the pinch of increased taxes. Many of the sons and daughters of these ranchers did not want to ranch or could not afford to buy their parents out. The Canadian dollar was high compared to the US dollar, giving Americans better purchasing power. After the Second World War, land was considerably cheaper in Canada than in the United States and purchasing ranches in British Columbia made good business sense. As well, few Canadian ranchers realized the substantial value of the timber on their ranches. One US buyer purchased a ranch for $500,000. Within a few years, he had taken out an equivalent amount in timber, leaving him with the property and animals for free. Unfortunately, many of the Americans who bought ranches in BC were businessmen first and cattlemen second. That meant that, while their business instincts were sharp, their understanding of ranching procedures and operations was limited. By the 1970s, two-thirds of the cattle land in the province was in the hands of Americans, many of whom did not live in BC.[1]

One of the first American entrepreneurs to see the potential in BC cattle ranches was William Phillip "Bill" Studdert. His father owned a fleet of boats and a cannery, and he started out as a deckhand on his father's fishing boats off the coast of Alaska. When his father died, Studdert inherited the cannery business and, by 1950, he had two freighters sailing between the United States and South America. Soon he branched out into the scrap metal industry and then into the livestock feed business. After the Second World War, he purchased the T Bar 3 Ranch in Phillipsburg, Montana, which covered 3,600 acres and ran 1,000 head of cattle. From there, he cast his eyes to British Columbia to look for a ranch that was relatively undervalued.

In 1948, Studdert and Floyd Skelton, a stockyard owner and auctioneer from Idaho Falls, Idaho, purchased the Gang Ranch from the Western Canadian Ranching Company, which had owned the ranch since 1888. It was rumoured that they paid $750,000. The Gang ran 6,000 head of cattle and 2,000 yearlings and, as was their practice in the T Bar 3, the new owners promptly sold off the majority of the ranch's breeding herd and yearlings to pay for the ranch. Bill Studdert moved into the elegantly decorated Big House near Gaspard Creek but the man who had spent most of his life on fishing boats wasn't known for his housekeeping habits. The beautiful house deteriorated and became infested with rats, mice and fleas. Studdert also gained a reputation for penny-pinching as he tried to squeeze as much profit as possible out of the operation without putting much back in. He was known for halving food orders for his cowboys and putting them on starvation diets and he did the same with his cattle. Eventually, Studdert decided to manage the ranch from an office in Ashcroft, 85 miles away from the ranch itself. Wages for the cowboys dropped and, when disgusted cowboys who had had enough decided to quit, they had to ride all the way to Ashcroft to collect their final cheque. The situation came to a head during the winter of 1957. Studdert, who was drinking more and more, disappeared in mid-summer and, without a manager to handle the haying crews, very little hay was put up for winter. Before winter had run its course, the ranch was out of hay and the cattle began to die off in record numbers. Skelton, finally having reached the end of his rope with Studdert, hired Melvin Sidwell, a successful potato farmer from Idaho, to manage the ranch. Sidwell soon realized that the ranch had lost most of its foundation herd, the heart of any ranching operation, and it had also done little to take advantage of new technology. Haying was still done by horses and what machinery the ranch had purchased lay broken and rusting from lack of maintenance; the ranch irrigation ditches and flumes had not been maintained and the hayfields were unproductive. Under Sidwell's management, the Gang Ranch fortunes began to improve. He rebuilt and improved the irrigation system and installed a water line from Freshwater Lake to provide running water to all the buildings. He planted a large acreage with potatoes to improve the land and was among the first in the province to plant corn for silage. Sidwell purchased machinery for haying and added a new steel calving barn and cement-block apartment building to house staff. He also added diesel generators to provide electricity to the ranch buildings and converted the heating systems from wood to oil, eliminating the use of year-round woodcutters. The Sidwell family remained on the Gang Ranch until 1975 and did much to turn around the decline of the vast operation, which at one time had been the largest cattle ranch in North America. In an effort to realize some return on the ranch, large parts of it were sold off, including the huge steer range north of the Chilcotin River, which was purchased by Neil Harvey, an Alberta rancher. This range was eventually incorporated into the Cotton Ranch. By the end of the Sidwell era the Gang Ranch was back on its feet again and operating in the black.

In his first years of managing the Gang Ranch, before the true result of his management became widely known, Bill Studdert was regarded as a fine example of good business management. Among his admirers was Victor Spencer, owner of the Diamond S Ranch across the Fraser River from the Gang Ranch. In 1950, Spencer and Studdert began to look at the other giant ranch in the province, the Douglas Lake Ranch, with an interest in buying. At the time, the ranch owned 143,250 acres and leased an additional 300,000 acres. This sustained a herd of around 10,000 head of cattle, a quarter of which were sold every year. Cattle prices were rising fast and, in 1949, cattle were bringing a record $192 a head, making the ranch a nice profit. Studdert and Spencer purchased the Douglas Lake Ranch in the summer of 1950 for $1.4 million. Spencer became president and Studdert, who was still very involved in the Gang Ranch, became managing director and vice-president. Brian Chance, who had taken over as ranch manager in 1940, was retained as manager.

Spencer and Studdert brought a distinctively different style of management to the Douglas Lake Ranch. As diehard free enterprisers, they were adamantly against using the BC Livestock Producers Cooperative Association for marketing their cattle. This was particularly awkward for Brian Chance, who was president of the co-operative. Studdert raced back and forth from the Gang to the Douglas Lake Ranch, pushing his cost-cutting measures and making Chance's job more and more difficult. Fortunately, Studdert's involvement in the ranch didn't last for long. By late 1950, Frank Ross, another friend of Victor Spencer, had expressed an interest in purchasing a share in the ranch. Ross was a successful businessman who had worked as director general of naval armaments and supply in Ottawa during the Second World War for a dollar a year. For his war service, he had been awarded a Companion of the Order of St. Michael and St. George from the British government.

Ross met with Spencer and Studdert and the three agreed to split the shares evenly. But Ross became concerned with Studdert's brash and uncaring ways and had second thoughts. He agreed to get involved on the stipulation that Bill Studdert have no part in the enterprise. After a marathon three-day negotiating session in Spencer's Vancouver office, Studdert agreed to relinquish his third of the ranch for a payout of $140,000, not bad considering he had put nothing down and had been involved for all of eight months.

However, if Brian Chance thought he was out of the woods with Studdert gone, he was in for a surprise. Spencer and Ross wanted to maximize their investment and demanded that the ranch sell 4,800 cows from the breeding stock on top of the normal sales of 3,000 head every year. This meant selling fully half of the herd each year, instead of a quarter. The only way to accomplish this was to sell the mature breeding cows and to breed all 1,500 of the yearling heifers instead of waiting until they were two-year-olds. The difficulty that young heifers have in delivering was reflected in the resulting annual losses of 6 percent of the cows and 18 percent of the calves. This was much higher than expected and the overall effect of these questionable measures was to reduce the size of the herd and especially the breeding stock that were essential to maintain quality and consistency. The sell-off of younger cattle was consistent with the new trend of sending yearlings to feedlots for finishing on grain, a practice that would soon become widespread. But, by 1953, the number of Douglas Lake yearlings available for sale was drastically reduced. Fortunately, the small number of ranch yearlings for sale coincided with the outbreak of hoof-and-mouth disease on the Prairies that saw the price of cattle drop by a third overnight.

The cost-cutting measures that Spencer and Ross had been pushing since their purchase of the ranch reached their pinnacle in 1953 when Brian Chance was instructed to not purchase any machinery or build any new buildings, fences or flumes. He had no other choice than to comply and watch the ranch deteriorate. When he successfully cut $100,000 from his expenses in 1953, he was rewarded by being told to reduce expenses further the next year.

By 1957, Spencer and Ross were beginning to realize what ranchers had known since the earliest days: that the rise and fall of cattle prices made it almost impossible to expect a profit every year and that, during times of depressed prices, it was best to cut your losses and hang on to your breeding stock. In the seven years that they had owned the ranch, profits had been marginal and the only way they had been able to pay off their initial investment was to sell off a large portion of their assets, namely the cattle. The two owners had certainly lost some of their enthusiasm for ranching and began to look for a purchaser. They approached Charles N. "Chunky" Woodward who, in partnership with a stockbroker friend, John J. West, agreed to purchase the ranch for $2.6 million. The Douglas Lake Cattle Company (1959) Limited was incorporated on June 24, 1959.

Grain-finished Beef

Up until the mid-1950s, the typical British Columbia Interior herd consisted of breeding stock, yearlings and two-year-olds, with occasional three-year-olds being marketed off the more isolated ranges. The cattle were marketed as two-year-olds finished on grass and shipped directly from the ranch, with most of them going by rail to the Greater Vancouver area from stockyards like those at Williams Lake. But a significant change took place in the ranching industry for all of western Canada in the mid-1950s. The year 1956 saw unprecedented grain surpluses on the Canadian Prairies that could only be disposed of as livestock feed. The resulting grain-finished beef was well received by consumers because the meat retained a brighter colour and remained firm with less leakage of moisture when packaged. Moreover, the fat tended to appear whiter in a grain-fed cow and maintained a fresher appearance. The resulting consumer demand was duly noted by large grocery chain stores, which began to market "grain-fed beef" as a superior product. This resulted in a market for "feeders" or young cattle that could be finished on grain. As a result, the demand for cattle finished on grass virtually disappeared.

The British Columbia Interior was not a grain-growing area and the cost of importing grain together with the expense of equipment for feeding meant that the vast majority of cattle had to be shipped to feedlots to be finished. By 1957, the demand for grain-finished rather than grass-finished beef meant that calves and yearlings were shipped to feed lots for finishing. Ranches only kept breeding stock, calves and "long yearlings." During 1957 and 1958, ranchers sold their grass-finished cattle as well as yearlings, until they could establish themselves on a "yearling basis." By the early 1960s, less than 10 percent of cattle were grass-finished and these animals were primarily in the Chilcotin, including the Gang Ranch, the Alkali Lake Ranch and the Chilco Ranch. But for most of the smaller ranches, to return to selling two-year-olds would have meant losing a year's income, which few could afford.

Before the mid-1950s, the typical herd would have consisted of one-third breeding stock (cows), one-third yearlings and one-third two-year-olds ready for market. But after the market changed to demanding younger feeder cattle, the composition of a herd was quite different. A herd of 400 cows would produce approximately 360 calves, of which 180 would be steers sold as calves or yearlings; of the remainder, 50 would be used as replacement heifers for the breeding herd and the remaining 130 heifers would be sold. The usual practice was to sell half the calf crop in the fall and winter, with the other half to be sold as "long yearlings" the following fall. The number of calves held over the winter would depend upon the market prices, the available winter-feed supply and the condition of the range.

There were a number of advantages to the marketing of yearling cattle for the ranchers of British Columbia. Because only mature breeding stock was kept on the ranches, calving was easier than when yearlings were left in the breeding herd. Also, because grass was no longer used for finishing cattle, the demands on precious grass resources were lessened. Where the lushest grassland areas had formerly been used to finish cattle before shipping them to market, the change to feedlot finishing meant that the best pastures could be saved for breeding time and calving.

Horseless Ranching

Haying

By the 1940s, ranches were beginning to look closely at motorized equipment, particularly for haying. At first, tractors were equipped with hay sweeps on the front to bring the hay to the stack. But the invention of the hay baler changed haying forever. The Guichon Ranch purchased the first baler in the Nicola Valley in 1944, a two-man Case baler. One man sat on the stationary baler and poked the hay wire through to the man on the other side, who tied it. Both positions were dusty and dirty but the one closest to the plunger was the worst. The man working there came out at the end of the day entirely green! The Guichon Ranch used that baler for the next five years.[2]

The early balers were stationary and had motors on them. But, as tractors improved, they had power takeoffs that could be used to run the baler. In 1947 the International Harvester Company came out with the first automatic string-tie baler, but the baler did not tie well and was not widely accepted. Eventually both New Holland and International Harvester came out with improved string-tie balers and they became accepted by ranchers all over the province. During the war years, when labour was scarce, the baler was the fastest and most effective way to get the hay into the barn or stack. Bales were easier to stack and balers did the work of six or seven men. At first, all the bales were hand-loaded onto racks pulled by teams of horses and taken to the haystack enclosure or barn where they were stacked, once again by hand. Before long, tractors pulling sleds were used to pick up bales and put them on a motorized conveyor to get into the barn or to the top of the haystack.

The Douglas Lake Ranch watched with interest at their neighbours', the Guichons, attempts to modernize the haying process. In the late 1940s, Douglas Lake purchased two Massey Harris Pony tractors to pull mowers at the Chapperon Lake hayfields but the 10-horsepower Pony proved to be a little underpowered. Once the swather was developed for cutting hay, the ranch replaced the Pony tractors with larger, more powerful tractors. The ranch slowly moved toward mechanization all through the 1940s. In 1946 it set up the Home Ranch machine shop and Laurie Graham became the ranch's first full-time mechanic. Prior to that, the ranch blacksmith had been responsible for all machinery repairs.

For the smaller ranches, haying with horses was still the most economical way to put up the winter hay. On the Mulvahill ranch near Chezacut, the ranch hands cut the hay with horse-drawn mowers and then contracted the Natives to stack the hay. The hay was valued per eight-foot ton, which is a stack of hay eight feet by eight feet by eight feet. Wild hay was looser in the stack and was paid for by the nine-foot ton. After the hay was stacked, Randolph Mulvahill would measure the width of the stack and then throw a rope over it and measure the overthrow to determine the square. Then he would measure the length of the stack to get the total volume. The Mulvahills used horses for haying right up until 1962 but most ranches made the transition to mechanized haying in the 1950s.

The Gang Ranch used horses for haying until the mid-1950s, partly because one of the ranch owners, Bill Studdert, refused to spend the money to mechanize. But when Melvin Sidwell took over managing the ranch in 1957, he purchased a Freeman square baler in Portland, Oregon, for use in the ranch hayfields. This baler was state of the art and extremely efficient. Unfortunately, it was not sold in Canada at the time and none of the BC dealerships stocked the twine needed to tie the bales. The twine had to be shipped up from Portland when it was required. While this was easily remedied by purchasing sufficient twine for a year's baling in the spring, it was a different matter if the baler broke down. Parts had to be shipped up from Portland as well, resulting in long periods of downtime while the crew sat and waited for a part to arrive.

The days of large haying crews and horse-drawn equipment were drawing to a close and those looking back on it experienced a certain sadness at witnessing the end of an era. Self-professed "pitchfork artist" Smokey Erlandson, who spent 25 years haying in the Kamloops area, reminisced: "Gazing at the lowly pitchfork, remembering the hard work associated with it, we also remember the good times and the laughs. At noon the crowning glory, after boiling a pot of tea, was to open the one big lunch bucket and see, staring us in the face, a loaf of bread, no butter, a sharp knife and enough salami for all. As this was cut up and passed around someone would usually remark. 'I wonder what the poor people are having for lunch!' Today my old pitchfork is used only for raking leaves and to lean on."[3]

Airplane Reconnaissance

Every fall on ranches all over North America, cowboys would round up the cattle and drive them from the high-country ranges down to the winter feed grounds. But, inevitably, some cattle were left behind, reluctant to come out as long as there was feed in the sheltered wooded areas. If these cattle were not rescued, they would eventually succumb to the cold and lack of feed and die, so cowboys would spend the late fall and early winter searching out these strays, incurring added expense and time. As wages climbed at the end of the war, ranchers began to look into another way of spotting lost cattle. There were thousands of returning airmen in the province, many of whom had purchased their own planes and were looking for a way to make them pay. It was economical and logical for ranchers to hire these bush pilots to fly over their high ranges and look for cattle from the air. They could communicate to cowboys on the ground by radio and the work of rounding up strays could be accomplished in a fraction of the time.

The bush pilots who flew these small planes over the remote ranch areas were always interested in a little adventure and were up for a challenge. Brian Chance found out the hard way just how adventurous they were. He was in the air with a pilot named Taylor when he had the idea of visiting Harry Chapman at Hatheume Lake. Since Hatheume was not completely frozen over, Taylor sat the plane down neatly on the frozen surface of nearby Ellen Lake and Chance had his visit. When they returned to the plane, its runners were frozen to the lake surface. At Taylor's command, Chance had to rock the plane until its skis were loose and then run alongside the moving plane and clamber into the cockpit. As if that wasn't enough, Chance sat in terror as the plane struggled to gain altitude and barely cleared the lodgepole pines ringing the lake. That experience kept Chance firmly on the ground for some time.

One of the pilots who did airplane reconnaissance for Bill Studdert of the Gang Ranch and other Cariboo and Chilcotin cattlemen was Les Kerr of Abbotsford. Kerr used the Clinton Hotel as his home base and would fly his spotter plane for any rancher who needed assistance. Studdert, who claimed to love to fly, would accompany him on his reconnaissance over the Gang Ranch. But Studdert seemed a little averse to actually looking out the window and kept his face buried in a newspaper the whole time he was in the air.

Trucking

The *Williams Lake Tribune* noted in 1952 for the first time, "The whine of trucks marks the path of the modern beef drive . . . This fall for the first time there will be no Big Creek cattle going to market on the hoof—no beef drive winding its leisurely way down the long dusty road to Williams Lake." Perhaps the most significant change in ranching during the 1950s was the trucking of cattle to market. Since the change to grain-finished beef meant that calves and yearlings instead of two- and three-year-olds were being sold to the buyers, it was easier on the cattle and on the rancher to load them into trucks and move them in a few hours over country that would have taken weeks if they were moved on the hoof. Even though the old cowhands maintained that the cattle lost more weight in a few hours on the trucks than they would in a week on the hoof, the end of the big cattle drives was in sight. When the ranchers reached the inevitable decision to move their cattle by truck, the trucks they picked were from Tommy Hodgson Trucking. Tommy had started out driving freight through the Chilcotin in 1914 and had battled almost impassible roads that would have made the average traveller faint dead away. In 1935, when the government built a road from the Chilco Ranch through to the Taylor Windfall Mine near Whitewater Lake, Tommy and his son, Wilf, drove the first truck of freight for the mine over the road. Two years later, Wilf took a 16,000-pound steel sharpener over the road by truck. The heavy load shifted and drove the sharpener partway through the cab of the truck but Hodgson still delivered it on time. When Tommy died in 1945, Wilf, in partnership with Joe Gillis, carried on Tommy Hodgson Trucking. So, when the first cattle trucks rolled into Williams Lake from the distant corners of the Chilcotin, it's not surprising that Hodgson trucks carried them.

Ranchers in the Cariboo began using trucks at the same time, but, as the PGE did not extend beyond Squamish until 1956, they preferred to truck their cattle to Ashcroft so they could be in Vancouver in another eight hours. This meant that the cattle could be more or less shipped to Vancouver from the Cariboo in a single day, allowing for a lot less shrinkage than any other method of shipping. Most ranchers constructed their own corrals and loading chutes so that the trucks could pull right up to them to load. It was generally believed that, as long as a cattle truck was moving and was loaded full of cattle, it was easy on the cattle. If the truck had to stop for any length of time, the cattle would become restless and move around, thereby losing weight. The advantage of trucking was that the cattle would arrive relatively fresh and not sore-footed and leg-weary as they inevitably did after the long drives. But most important was how much time was saved by trucking them.

Even though horses were no longer being used for farm work, there was always a need for good saddle horses for cow work. By the 1950s, the quarter horse was beginning to attract interest among the ranchers of British Columbia. The first quarter horses in the province were brought in by Art Hay, manager of the Nicola Lake Stock Farm, in 1953. He brought in 18 horses, including 2 stallions, from Texas and Ellensburg, Washington. Hay boasted that the quarter horse could "turn on a two bit piece and give you back 24 cents change." The quarter horse's agility was certainly an asset in cutting cattle out of a herd.

The Last of the Big Cattle Drives

The ease of trucking cattle to market or to shipping points made long cattle drives a thing of the past. But there were still occasions when there was no choice but to move cattle overland on the hoof. One of these times was in the spring of 1951 when Gang Ranch owner/manager, Bill Studdert, wanted 1,000 yearling steers and heifers driven from the Perry Ranch, east of Cache Creek, to the Gang Ranch. To head up the drive, he hired Harry Marriott, who had sold his Big Bar Creek ranch the year before. Marriott was an experienced cattleman who had started out as a cowboy for the Gang Ranch 40 years before and knew the country between the two ranches very well. He knew he would need good, experienced cowboys for the drive, so he spent some time at the Gang Ranch getting together saddle horses and having them shod, organizing supplies and getting to know the available cowboys.

On a bright spring morning, Marriott left the Gang Ranch with a wagon pulled by a team of horses and filled with supplies, tents and bedrolls, in company with two cowboys and a cook who was married to one of the cowboys. After two and a half days' travel, they reached the Perry Ranch where the cattle were spread out across the sagebrush flats and on the nearby mountain. Marriott's cowboys were joined by several cowboys who had been part of the Perry Ranch crew to round up the cattle. It took a few days to round up all the cattle and Marriott noted that some of them were in poor condition, which was surprising as there were stacks of hay still standing on the ranch. It looked like the rumours of Studdert's penny-pinching ways were well founded. About 75 head of the cattle did not appear capable of making the long overland trek, so Marriott left them behind. Once they left the ranch, the first part of the cattle drive was over the Cariboo Road, which was by now a paved highway. To avoid traffic, Marriott would start the drive as early as possible in the morning after Maude, the cook, had provided them with a breakfast of coffee, hot bannock and mulligan.

By the end of the third day, the drive had arrived at the outskirts of Clinton and Marriott intended to be up before dawn to drive the cattle through town before anyone was up in the morning. A few Clinton residents protested that the cattle would leave their "cow chips" on their main street and make a mess but, as Marriott pointed out, "it's these old chips and the folks that have to live by them are the only things that ever kept this town and country going all these years and without them, this whole district couldn't have made a living."[4] The cattle were gently moved through Clinton with only the town dogs to contend with and, by 4:30 a.m., they were heading north on the highway.

The long climb out of Clinton was difficult for the cattle, which were growing tired from the daily trek, so they were moved slowly and were not pushed at all. It was a challenge to keep the thirsty cattle from rushing to the sloughs alongside the road. The bottoms of these sloughs were deep mud and would mire an animal. The cattle inevitably rushed to the shore to drink and, sure enough, some would wade out and get stuck, and the cowboys would have to rope them and drag them out. Finally the cattle and cowboys reached 57 Mile House, where their route turned off the Cariboo highway. The cattle were rested for a day and then pushed westward through the flat open country to Meadow Lake. The grass was abundant along this route, there having been few cattle over it for some time. The cattle were well fed and grew stronger each day.

At Meadow Lake, Bill Studdert arrived to tell Marriott to split the drive in half, keeping one half at Meadow Lake and driving the other half to the Crow's Bar area on the Gang Ranch across the Fraser River. Those at Meadow Lake were taken through to the Gang Ranch a couple of weeks later. On completion of the drive, Marriott remarked, "I think that it is the last time that I ever heard of any worthwhile drive on the road, and it was my last effort in that line. It would have been a far better success, and way less aggravating, if the cattle had been fat beef cattle, instead of half-fed and thin doggies, with not enough fat on them to grease the hinges of a pair of spectacles." Marriott returned to the Gang Ranch a couple of years later and noticed, "I saw some of these steers two years later and you'd never have recognized them, after being so weak and thin, but that old bunch-grass is better than all the vitamin pills rolled into one."[5]

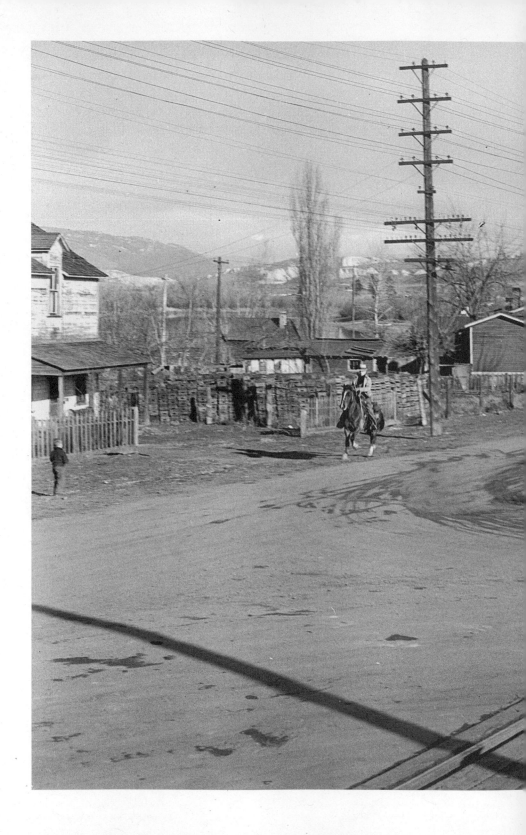

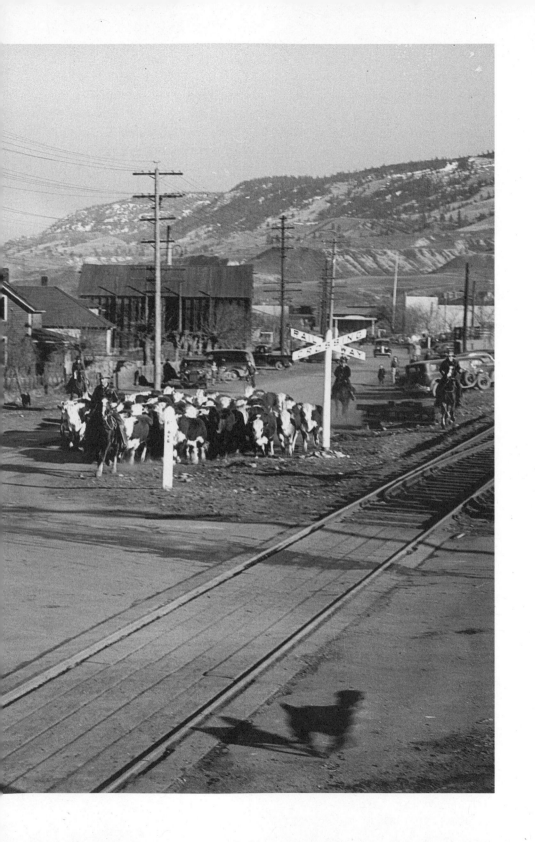

One of the last ranching areas in the British Columbia Interior to drive cattle to market was the Nazko area east of Quesnel. As late as 1954, ranchers were still driving their cattle to the stockyards in Quesnel, 62 miles to the east. The drive, which took most of the summer, started in the most remote areas and picked up additional cattle at each ranch along the way. The distant ranches would head their cattle out by mid-April and spend until mid-September on the trail. Since most of the ranches were small, family-run operations, the entire family would often head out on the drive. Ranchers would hire a few cowboys, mostly Natives from the Nazko Reserve, to drive the cattle or they would hire the Natives to put up hay if they stayed with their cattle through the drive. The ranchers had camp wagons or pack horses to carry their supplies and bedding so that they could camp out each night. The cattle were moved only a few miles a day so that they could feed and come into Quesnel in as good shape as possible for auction. By the time the cattle reached the west side of the Fraser River at Quesnel, there were several hundred head milling about. Crossing the bridge was a challenge as any more than 10 head at one time would push the old bridge to its breaking point. The cowboys would string the cattle out and push them across the wooden deck a few at a time before heading them through town to the stockyards next to the PGE railway station and yards. The cattle were auctioned off there and then loaded onto cattle cars for their trip to the coast.

After five months on the trail, and with their pay in their pockets, the cowboys would let loose as they filled the Quesnel hotels and bars. The RCMP would stand by and step in if things got out of hand but would try to let the men have their fun. On Friday and Saturday nights, the doors of the beer parlours would be closed to entry or exit once things got going. If a cowboy chose to leave, he was not allowed back in. This practice contained the mayhem to some extent.

Once the partying was over, the ranchers and cowboys would prepare to head back into the bush. In most cases, it would be another year before they got to town again so they had to purchase all the supplies they needed for the year to come. They loaded their wagons to the hilt with food, tools and other necessities for the long trip back home and said goodbye to the city. Quesnel merchants said their goodbyes with mixed feelings. Their pockets were full of the cattle auction proceeds but they were content to wait another year before going through it all again!

(preceding pages) Driving cattle through the streets of Kamloops, 1947. Ranchers tried to move their cattle early in the morning to avoid slowing traffic. *Royal BC Museum, BC Archives photo I-29155*

By the mid-1950s, long cattle drives to market were over forever in the British Columbia Interior. The cattle industry was changing and the time-honoured ways of ranching were drawing to a close. Cattle drives had been the accepted way of moving cattle since the first bovines were domesticated. The men and women who had been involved in these drives had developed ways of moving cattle that, though they had evolved in some ways, remained much the same over time. Whether it was old men and boys on foot driving cattle with dogs and whips in the hills of Britain or mounted men in the salt marshes of southern Spain, the principles were the same. Move the cattle slowly so they can eat on the way and not lose weight. Count your cattle morning and evening and, if some are missing, your priority is to find them, for cattle represent money. Let the strong cattle take the lead and the weaker, slower ones follow behind, but always keep your drove together. If you need to, slow down the lead cattle because strung-out cattle can be difficult to control. If these basic principles are observed, the cattle will arrive at market in no worse shape than when you started out. Then the drover, cowboy, cow puncher or buckaroo can rest easy and feel a sense of accomplishment in a job well done.

ENDNOTES

Chapter One: The Great War

1. Bulman, *Kamloops Cattlemen*, p. 54.
2. Adams, *The Old-time Cowhand*, p. 302.
3. Bonner et al., *Chilcotin*, pp. 54–55.
4. *Williams Lake Tribune*, March 12, 1953.
5. Boam and Brown, *British Columbia*, p. 396.
6. Alvin Johnston, "Birchbark to Steel," (unpublished manuscript), 1959.
7. Woolliams, *Cattle Ranch*, pp. 164–66.
8. Place, *Dog Creek*, p. 124.
9. Both the "lower farm" and the "upper farm," near Mission Creek, were originally owned by William Pinchbeck, who constructed a two-storey house on the lower property and a roadhouse on the upper one. The Western Ranching Company took over from Pinchbeck and sold the entire property to Bob Borland who operated the "lower" ranch himself and leased the upper ranch to Mike Minton, a Chilcotin rancher.
10. Heritage Committee, *Bunch Grass to Barbed Wire*, p. 152.
11. Ibid., p. 211.
12. Bonner et al., *Chilcotin*, p. 199.
13. For further reading, see Ken Mather's *Buckaroos and Mud Pups*.
14. Stangoe, *Looking Back at the Cariboo–Chilcotin with Irene Stangoe*, pp. 65–67.
15. Marriott, *Cariboo Cowboy*, p. 79.
16. Bonner et al., *Chilcotin*, p. 96.
17. Marriott, *Cariboo Cowboy*, p. 72.
18. Woolliams, *Cattle Ranch*, p. 126.

Chapter Two: Boom Years

1. Bulman, *Kamloops Cattlemen*, p. 58.
2. Lavington, *Born to Be Hung*, p. 22.
3. Ibid., pp. 30–31.
4. Cox, *Ranching*, p. 81.
5. Stangoe, *Cariboo–Chilcotin*, p. 40.
6. Quoted in Bonner et al., *Chilcotin*, p. 100.
7. Bulman, *Kamloops Cattlemen*, p. 56.
8. Peg Marriott, interview by Hilda Mortimer, 197-?, interview T2725:0001, Royal BC Museum, BC Archives, Victoria BC.
9. *Calgary Herald*, May 29, 1967.
10. Cox, *Ranching*, p. 192.
11. Marriott, *Cariboo Cowboy*, p. 73.
12. Cox. *Ranching*, p. 157.
13. Gordon Parke, interview by the author, September 2009.
14. Cox, *Ranching*, p. 152.
15. Ibid., p. 147.
16. Bunch Trudeau, interview by Imbert Orchard, July 20, 1968, interview T1783:0001, Royal BC Museum, BC Archives, Victoria BC.
17. Ibid.
18. Jack Durrell, interview by Derek Lawrence Reimer and John Allan Roberts, 1976, interview T0594:0001, Royal BC Museum, BC Archives, Victoria BC.

Chapter Three: Bust Years

1. Marriott, *Cariboo Cowboy*, p. 104.
2. Bulman, *Kamloops Cattlemen*, p. 139.
3. Woolliams, *Cattle Ranch*, p. 139.
4. Cox, *Ranching*, p. 146.
5. Heritage Committee, *Bunch Grass to Barbed Wire*, p. 77.
6. Marriott, *Cariboo Cowboy*, p. 134.
7. Ibid., pp. 134, 156.
8. Heritage Committee, *Bunch Grass to Barbed Wire*, p. 217.
9. Martha Furrer, interview by Debra Ireland, August 2, 1979, interview T4164:0007, Royal BC Museum, BC Archives, Victoria BC.
10. Lavington, *The Nine Lives of a Cowboy*, p. 98.
11. Cox, *Ranching*, p. 130.
12. Bulman, *Kamloops Cattlemen*, p. 129.
13. Cox, *Ranching*, p. 131

14. Young, ed., *Quelle Grande Prairie*, p. 186.
15. Miller, *Haying with Horses*, p. 87.
16. Bulman, *Kamloops Cattlemen*, p. 131.
17. Cox, *Ranching*, p. 68.
18. Ibid., p. 196.
19. Ibid., p. 241.
20. Thomas, *Fifty Years, Three and a Half Million Cattle*, p. 12.
21. Marriott, *Cariboo Cowboy*, p. 176.
22. Ibid., p. 104.
23. Jack Durrell, interview by Derek Lawrence Reimer and John Allan Roberts, 1976, interview T0594:0001, Royal BC Museum, BC Archives, Victoria BC.
24. Marriott, *Cariboo Cowboy*, p. 133.
25. Place, *Dog Creek*, p. 169.
26. Bonner et al., *Chilcotin*, pp. 139–41.
27. Ibid., p. 157.
28. Marriott, *Cariboo Cowboy*, p. 137.
29. Heritage Committee, *Bunch Grass to Barbed Wire*, p. 21.
30. Bonner et al., *Chilcotin*, p. 155.
31. Logan, *Dog Creek*, pp. 140, 172.
32. Cox, *Ranching*, p. 224.

Chapter Four: Winds of War

1. Bulman, *Kamloops Cattlemen*, p. 163.
2. Woolliams, *Cattle Ranch*, p. 173.
3. Marriott, *Cariboo Cowboy*, p. 168.
4. Cox, *Ranching*, p. 29.
5. Bonner et al., *Chilcotin*, p. 204.
6. Stangoe, *Looking Back at the Cariboo–Chilcotin with Irene Stangoe*, pp. 33–35.
7. Stangoe, *History and Happenings in the Cariboo–Chilcotin*, pp. 64–69.
8. Woolliams, *Cattle Ranch*, p. 170.
9. Bonner et al., *Chilcotin*, p. 259.
10. Bulman, *Kamloops Cattlemen*, p. 119.
11. Ibid., p. 105.
12. Ferguson, *Cowboys, Good Times & Wrecks*, p. 10.
13. Cox, *Ranching*, p. 167.
14. Marriott, *Cariboo Cowboy*, p. 163.
15. Thomas, *Fifty Years, Three and a Half Million Cattle*, p. 30.

16. Woolliams, *Cattle Ranch*, p. 175.
17. Bulman, *Kamloops Cattlemen*, p. 160.
18. *The Canadian Encyclopedia*, Volume IV, p. 2255.
19. Cox, *Ranching*, p. 102.
20. Young, *Quelle Grande Prairie*, p. 114.

Chapter Five: A New Era Dawns
1. Gould, *Ranching in Western Canada*, p. 139.
2. Cox, *Ranching Now, Then, and Way Back When*, p. 172.
3. Heritage Committee, *Bunch Grass to Barbed Wire*, p. 71.
4. Marriott, *Cariboo Cowboy*, p. 191.
5. Ibid, p. 193.

REFERENCES

Published Sources

Adams, Ramon F. *The Old-time Cowhand*. New York: The Macmillan Co., 1961.

Boam, H.J. and A.G. Brown. *British Columbia*. London, England: Sells Ltd., 1912.

Bonner, Veera, Irene Bliss and Hazel Henry Litterick. *Chilcotin: Preserving Pioneer Memories*. Surrey, BC: Heritage House, 1995.

Bulman, T. Alex. *Kamloops Cattlemen: One Hundred Years of Trail Dust*. Winlaw, BC: Sono Nis Press, 1972.

Cox, Doug. *Ranching: Now, Then and Way Back When*. Penticton, BC: Skookum Publications, 2004.

Ferguson, Pat. *Cowboys, Good Times & Wrecks*. Clearwater, BC: Fergie's Follies, 2007.

Forbes, Molly. *Lac la Hache: Historical Notes on the Early Settlers*. Quesnel, BC: Big Country Printers, n.d.

Gould, Ed. *Ranching in Western Canada*. Saanichton, BC: Hancock House Publishers, 1978.

Harris, Lorraine. *Halfway to the Goldfields: A History of Lillooet*. Vancouver, BC: J.J. Douglas Ltd., 1977.

Heritage Committee, *Bunch Grass to Barbed Wire . . . just a little south of Kamloops*. Knutsford, BC: Rosehill Farmers Institute, 1984.

Lavington, H. "Dude." *Born to be Hung*. Winlaw, BC: Sono Nis Press, 1983.

——. *The Nine Lives of a Cowboy*. Winlaw, BC: Sono Nis Press, 1982.

Logan, Don. *Dog Creek: 100 Years*. Victoria, BC: Trafford Publishing, 2007.

Marriott, Harry. *Cariboo Cowboy*. Sidney, BC: Gray's Publishing, 1966.

Mather, Ken. *Buckaroos and Mud Pups: The early days of ranching in British Columbia*. Surrey, BC: Heritage House, 2006.

Miller, Lynn R. *Haying with Horses*. Sisters, Oregon: Small Farmer's Journal, 2000.

Patenaude, Branwen. *Trails to Gold*. Surrey, BC: Heritage House, 1995.

——. *Trails to Gold Volume Two: Roadhouses of the Cariboo*. Surrey, BC: Heritage House, 1996.

Place, Hilary. *Dog Creek: A Place in the Cariboo*. Surrey, BC: Heritage House, 1999.

Selody, Marjorie M. *Meeting of the Winds: A History of Falkland*. Vernon, BC: Wayside Press, 1990.

Stangoe, Irene. *Cariboo–Chilcotin: Pioneer People and Places*. Surrey, BC: Heritage House, 1994.

——. *History and Happenings in the Cariboo–Chilcotin*. Surrey, BC: Heritage House, 2000.

——. *Looking Back at the Cariboo–Chilcotin with Irene Stangoe*. Surrey, BC: Heritage House, 1997. (Based on the unfinished manuscript of the late Carol Shaw.)

Thomas, Morrie. *Fifty Years, Three and a Half Million Cattle: A History of the B.C. Livestock Producers Co-operative Association: Commemorating Fifty Years of Service to the Livestock Industry of British Columbia, 1943–1993*. Kamloops, BC: BC Livestock Producers Co-operative Association, 1993.

Weir, Thomas. "Ranching in the Southern Interior Plateau of British Columbia." Department of Mines and Technical Surveys. Ottawa, Ontario: Queen's Printer, 1964.

Woolliams, Nina G. *Cattle Ranch: The Story of the Douglas Lake Cattle Company*. Vancouver, BC: Douglas & McIntyre, 1979.

Young, Margaret F. *Quelle Grande Prairie: History of Grande Prairie, Adelphi and Westwold*. Vernon, BC: Wayside Press, 1994.

Archival Sources

Historic O'Keefe Ranch
Johnston, Alvin. "Birchbark to Steel." unpublished manuscript, 1959.
Museum of the Cariboo Chilcotin, Williams Lake
Okanagan Archives Trust Society
Royal BC Museum, BC Archives (formerly known as Provincial Archives of BC)

Newspapers and Periodicals

Calgary Herald.
Nicola Valley Historical Quarterly 1–5. (1977–1983).
Vancouver Sun.
Williams Lake Tribune.

Ken Mather has been involved in researching, writing and interpreting western Canadian heritage for over three decades. He started out as a researcher for Fort Edmonton Park in 1973. In 1979, Ken moved to BC to work at Barkerville Historic Park; he became the park's curator in 1982. From 1984 until 2004 he was the manager/ curator of the Historic O'Keefe Ranch near Vernon, BC, where he developed his love of early cowboy history. Ken is now the general manager of Historic Hat Creek Ranch, near Cache Creek.

Also by Ken Mather

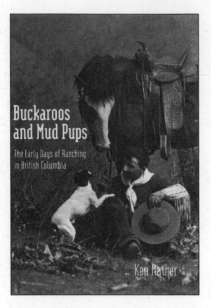

Buckaroos and Mud Pups

The Early Days of Ranching in
British Columbia

978-1-894974-09-7
$19.95

Remarkable cattle drives, famous ranches and legendary characters are at the
heart of Ken Mather's first book about ranching in BC. The story begins in the
1860s, the start of a decade that saw more than 22,000 head of cattle brought
into the colony, and continues through to 1914, by which time ranching in
the B.C. interior had become big business.

Ken introduces drovers, ranchers, cowboys and "mud pups" (the remittance
men of the ranching industry). Meet Jim "Big Kid" Madden, "BC Cattle King"
Johnny Wilson, the flamboyant Harper brothers and many others in this
entertaining look at fascinating times and the people who made them so.

www.heritagehouse.ca